THUS TO REVISIT . . .

THUS TO REVISIT...

by

JAMES AGATE

LONDON
HOME & VAN THAL LTD.
1947

MADE AND PRINTED IN GREAT BRITAIN
BY THE STANHOPE PRESS LIMITED
ROCHESTER : : KENT

To

J. B. PRIESTLEY

My thanks are due to all those publishers who had the courage to print these essays in the first place, and to whose courtesy I am indebted for permission to reprint them here.

NOTE

THE earliest essay in this little collection was written in 1917; the latest in 1942. I have deliberately left in phrases like "last week" and "on Monday night". My thanks are due to Mr. Frank Dunn for his kindness in correcting the proofs.

London 1947   J.A.

Contents

Player's Progress

〜〜〜〜〜〜〜〜〜〜〜〜〜〜〜〜〜〜〜〜〜〜〜〜〜

A STATE of ecstasy is to be reckoned among the more generous lapses, an error on the magnificent side. Writes the great French poet of his brother-visionaries:

> "Tous nos palais sous eux s'éteignent et s'affaissent;
> Leur âme à la coupole où leur œuvre reluit
> Revole, et ce ne sont que leurs corps qu'ils nous laissent.

> "Notre jour leur paraît plus sombre que la nuit;
> Leur œil cherche toujours le ciel bleu de la fresque,
> Et le tableau quitté les tourmente et les suit.

> "Comme Buonarotti, le peintre gigantesque,
> Ils ne peuvent plus voir que les choses d'en haut,
> Et que le ciel de marbre où leur front touche presque.
> Sublime aveuglement! magnifique défaut!"

A pardonable blindness, a magnificent fault, you may say, when levelled against a Michael Angelo; less easily pardonable when charged to the account of the mountebank and vagabond. Which of these notoriety-mongers, you will ask, was ever blind except to his own artistic deficiencies, or less than supremely awake to the crowd yoked to his triumphal car?

In the arts it is not always easy to give plain answers to plain questions. Criticism of the actor would be simpler were it not for the rehearsed quality of his emotion. At the moment of delivery the actor is essentially less interested than the spectator. It is not to be thought that the preoccupation of Buonarotti when he descended the scaffolding of the Sistine Chapel was less than the wonder of the first beholder; it is unthinkable that the great Dumas, rushing in tears out of his study with the exclamation, "J'ai tué Porthos!" was less moved than his reader. But the Othello whose demand to be roasted in sulphur and washed in steep-down gulfs of liquid fire should be heart-felt would not be able to sustain the rôle for a week. We may have to refer again to this old paradox of the insincerity of acting. As for its vulgarity, look around.

9

Look around not, for politeness' sake, at the living but at the illustrious dead. Consider the departed glory of renowned actresses little other than courtesans, some indeed not so warm-hearted; consider the luxury and insolence, the selfishness and feather-headedness—*étourderie* is the word—let the poet soften these vices as he may.

> "Cœur d'ange et de lion, libre oiseau de passage,
> Espiègle enfant ce soir, sainte artiste demain."

Consider whether, on hearing of an actor that he was a shy and modest gentleman, courteous towards others and a stranger to show and vanity, we should not on this report decide against him as a world-shaking virtuoso. And whether, on hearing of another that he was ill-mannered, vicious, moody, raffish, impulsive, ostentatious, egotistical, vain, we should be astonished to learn that he was, in the old phrase, an ornament to the stage. The French accept this contradiction readily. Let but a man prove wanting in honour, faith, friendship, and common honesty, and they cheerfully proclaim him "un comédien". And the proclamation is held to be dispensatory of all necessity for further judgment. The category suffices. We English are convinced something against our will of this divorce of genius from character. "The most tragic thing in the world," says Mr. Shaw's bedside raisonneur, "is a man of genius who is not also a man of honour." And yet when we read of Fanny Kemble and Rachel, we claim for the Victorian lady that she was a charming and gentle actress, and grudgingly admit for the Frenchwoman that she could undoubtedly play Phèdre. With all this, the French reverence for the actor's art is undoubtedly greater than our own, though they make short work of any of the actor's pretensions in his private capacity. We knight our rogues and vagabonds; the French dub them "cabotins", with all that word connotes of tawdry finery and fifth-rate plumage.

"What reasons, then, can you give for claiming a state of spiritual ecstasy for your mountebank?" is a question one must be prepared to answer. I am inclined to say of this suspect and theatrical ecstasy what I would say of all the other artistic elations—that it is the original ecstasy of creation, all great acting being creative in the sense that if there is one glory of Dickens's Micawber and another glory of the same character according to Phiz, so also is there one glory of Molière's Bourgeois Gentilhomme and another of Coquelin's M. Jourdain. By ecstasy I mean the original creative energy, imaginative fire and thought of a first fashioning, the laying-up in the actor's brain of a first store of imaginative effort from which to supply the minute doles required of mechanical performance. This quantity of imagination is constant, since the amount of renewed feeling which the actor necessarily brings even to rehearsed delivery can be relied upon to make good the wastage of original treasure.

And how, it may be asked, is this creation of original ecstasy so determined that we may be sure that it is a matter of imaginative fire and quickening thought and not merely of careful diligence and assidu-ity? It will save a good deal of trouble if we lay it down once and for all that hard work by itself will no more kindle imaginative fire than the taking of pains, however infinite, will add up in the end to a score of genius. Whatever the rude sage may have said, genius was never the affair of accountancy. On the other hand, imagination is powerless without technical training. I do not know which is the more deplorable spectacle, the London leading-lady who has learnt to fold up a parasol, sink into a chair, and preside over the tea-cups with a distinction of manner concealing an intelligence less than a midinette's, or the actress so taken up with her spirituality that she has scorned to learn the mechanical business of how to walk and sit. The old tag that Garrick "stepped upon the stage a master of his art" is responsible for an enor-mous amount of mischief in its encouragement to the actor to believe that he may rival Garrick by sheer virtuosity of the intelligence. Where-as the plain truth is that with the business of acting—the sheer power of pretending to be somebody else—brains have never had and never will have anything to do. Wherever the theorist writes "intellect" it is safe to read "temperament". There is a little verse by Théodore de Banville which exemplifies this need for technical preparation:

"Sculpteur, cherche avec soin, en attendant l'extase,
    Un marbre sans défaut pour en faire un beau vase . . ."

In other words, the actor must busy himself with furbishing up his technical armoury *en attendant l'extase*, awaiting such time as it shall please the divine fire to descend upon him.

To define the flame of ecstasy is to go back to the first principles of all art. Shortly we may allege the passionate quest for beauty; the search for light that never was on sea or land; the expression of all that some mysterious madness has taught the artist to be supremely worth while-setting down in word or paint or sound; the effort to

11

perpetuate beyond the grave and in terms of his art that consciousness of the world about him which has been said to be civilised man's "marvel and treasure". It is the love of work brought to perfection in a garret and on a crust. It is persistence in the face of neglect. Fame and applause are fuel to the vanity of the artist; the flame of ecstasy burns a spiritual oil. There is no tragedian of the Shakespearian stage, no comedian ripe with Molière and charged with character like a bursting grape, no maker of faces at the Palais-Royal who has not lighted his lamp at this serene and steady light.

And yet there is something of the Will o' the Wisp about this ecstatic candle of ours. We must, of course, be careful not to allow the actor who has failed to master the elementary tricks of his profession to humbug us by hiding his incompetence under a bushel of pretended inflation. The audience has nothing to do with the communings between the actor and his soul; they are purely the actor's affair. It may even be that where the actor is most consciously ecstatic he is least successful. There was a distinguished player once who professed inability to deliver Vincentio's

"Look, the unfolding star calls up the shepherd,"

unless he first visualised Watts' picture of Hope. To which a critic replied that the spur and inspiration of the actor are irrelevant, and that the business of acting, like the plumber's, is satisfactory only in so far as it is practical. "What the plumber thinks about is no concern of ours, until he translates it into terms of pipes." Between these two extremes ecstasy must find a mean.

Perhaps it will help to an understanding if we consider ecstasy on a humbler level. Once in a sporting paper I happened on a definition which all the thinking I have done since has not been able to better. The writer was describing a Welsh pony: "A veritable Ganymede in form, Shooting Star has action which, when seen, makes life easier for the man who loves fine horses and fine action." Makes life easier, there's the whole secret! The action of one little pony made life easier for this penny-a-liner, made him for the rapturous moment indifferent to ill-health, bankruptcy, the world's peace even. It is the business of great actors to make life easier. There is an old saying which describes people as being above themselves, and we remember that Galsworthy gave his charwoman a phrase for her drunken husband—"He isn't himself." The business of great acting is to raise the spectator above

12

himself, to intoxicate him, so that he is raised to a power of appreciation undreamed of in his sober senses. In this way the ecstasy in the artist speaks to the ecstasy which is in all of us.

It does not do to lay down too hard and fast a rule as to what shall or shall not elate a man above his normal self. The old Yorkshire proverb that there are trimmings for all sorts of cloth and buttons for fustian is true of the things of the spirit also. You cannot predict what will make life easier for the individual. I have been present at camp concerts where soldier-sentiment has stirred one's heart more than the masterpieces. I have seen an arch and fleshy singer—oh, the archness of forty!—hold in cathedral silence a crowded music-hall notoriously profane. I have seen two plump females and a dress-coated counter-jumper, halo'd with blue, amber, and pink lights, draw with trombone, flute, and violin more tears from Godard's "Berceuse" than ever that sentimental composer dreamed of putting into it. All these trumpery ballads made life easier for many simple souls. They have as good a right to be considered challenges to ecstasy as, in different degree, the clown twisting his apron as the curtain falls on *Sumurùn*, the negro page in *Rosenkavalier* prolonging the melody by a coda that he may pick up the dropped handkerchief, Samuel Butler's likening of Handel's "And the government shall be upon his shoulder" to the shoulder of the Wetterhorn, the "Holà! holà! que fais-tu là à la fenêtre?" of Sarah Bernhardt in *Pelléas et Mélisande*. It is the business of criticism to discriminate between these ecstasies, without superciliousness and without losing its head.

If, then, the attitude of the actor towards his creation is properly one of reverence, it is fitting that in his turn the spectator should abase himself before the glorious conception. But it is in no way desirable that he should prostrate himself before the actor in the flesh. In the immensely amusing *Les Grotesques de la Musique* of Hector Berlioz— a sane and witty corrective which should be at the elbow of every critic—there is a long description of the attitude towards its favourites assumed by the public of that day. Berlioz postulates an admirer of Jenny Lind who, with some notion of preserving at least an appearance of mental balance, should indulge in no more extravagant a pæan than "Goddess, I am to implore your pardon on behalf of a stunted humanity for its inability to find words adequate to its emotions. Your voice has the sublimity of the Heavenly Choir. Your beauty is beyond compare, your genius boundless, your trill more amazing than the sun. Saturn's ring is unworthy to crown your head. Before you humanity can but prostrate itself; deign at least that it embrace your feet." In reply to which poverty-stricken meed the incensed diva, with a shrug of her beautiful shoulders, demands, "What noodle have we here?"

The diarist, claiming for the great Kean's Sir Giles Overreach that it caused maidens to swoon and matrons to be untimely delivered in the pit did no more than faintly adumbrate the belief of world-shaking actors in their power actually to shake the world. We may, if we like, attribute this megalomania to the fleeting nature of the actor's triumph and his desire to seize the palm while yet it may be worn. Far from playing for posterity, far even from envisaging the considered verdict of the morrow, the actor demands the instantaneous applause of the moment. He who is to shake worlds must scatter his thunder-bolts within three feet of his judges, shut up with them in the stuffy box of false sentiment and vitiated atmosphere which is the theatre. We might take a more charitable view of the actor were his art other than a calculated simulation, a rigorous abstention from the stimulant which it is his business to administer critically, in rehearsed doses, maintaining behind his false face an air of eager participation. The actor is a giver of banquets of which it is the prime condition that the host shall abstain. Needs must, to borrow a phrase from Lamb, that he "sit esurient at his own table". "We're doing the trick, Charles, we're doing the trick!" whispered towards the close of his career by the elder Kean to the younger in I know not what pathetic play of stage-father kneeling to stage-son, is good enough to be the classic instance of ecstasy laughing up its sleeve—charlatanism, in a word. To be reckoned amongst the most poignant demonstrations of the pathos of human intercourse, and amongst the most intolerable exhibitions measured in any scale of æsthetic propriety, was the last public appearance of that always capable and occasionally exquisite actor, Frank Rodney, stricken with a mortal complaint. The impropriety consisted in the dying man's choice for his farewell of the rôle of Buckingham in *Henry VIII*:

> "You few that loved me,
> And dare be bold to weep for Buckingham,
> His noble friends and fellows, whom to leave
> Is only bitter to him, only dying,
> Go with me, like good angels, to my end,"

14

drew forth no tears for Buckingham, although every eye in the house was wet for Rodney. At the last words:

> "All good people,
> Pray for me! I must now forsake ye: the last hour
> Of my long weary life is come upon me.
> Farewell!
> And when you would say something that is sad,
> Speak how I fell. I have done; and God forgive me!"

men and women cried openly and the house was choked with heartfelt and unlawful sobs. . . .

Actors themselves are the first to recognise that the doubling of substance and shadow is not closer than that of tragedian and buffoon. A great French actress, wearied by a young gentleman's commendations of l'Aiglon's dying cry of "Maman!" exclaimed with just impatience: "Mais, mon petit, vous devez avoir bien remarqué qu'à ce moment-là tout le monde pleure, tousse, crache, se mouche et cetera, et cetera. Eh bien! je le fais exprès pour avoir un instant de repos!"

A charming actress, whose art is as English as the heroines of Shakespeare, condemned on occasion to some crude drama of the Terror, was ushered into a room overlooking the place of execution. In luxurious abandonment to the most trying emotions—a scene of poignant dissembling—she awaited in agony the advent in tumbrils of the greater part of her family. To her entered an attendant, saying, "This, Madam, is your apartment". Through tears, and in a voice which had melted continents, came on one light-hearted occasion the sotto voce reply, "I trust there are the usual conveniences!" Is it to be supposed that by such levity and "insincerity" Ellen Terry forfeited one-millionth shade of a degree of our reverence? I have the story on the authority of Courtenay Thorpe, who played the attendant.

Actors there are who plead that they would be glad enough to be artists if the public would only let them. Again one has to quote Berlioz, who, writing somewhere of Madame Sontag, says that she was the only singer of his day who would risk her reputation by singing *piano*. Berlioz goes on to declare that a *piano*, a *pianissimo* even, can be got for the asking out of an orchestra a hundred strong or a choir double the number (an orchestra, like any other composite body, has neither soul to save nor backside to kick), but that from the diva, be she clever or unskilful, intelligent or stupid, human or divine, no *piano* is obtainable by flattery or threat, cajolery or whiplash. That Berlioz was right in his time those will concede who realise how rare, even to-day, in the speaking theatre, is the actor who will subordinate himself, who will allow that his rôle can have its diminuendos as well as its crescendos. "Vous avez bien fait de venir m'entendre ce soir," exclaimed a great French actress after a particularly fine performance. "Dieu même me soufflait." A forfanterie with the implication that on occasion the divine fire might be lacking.

I remember a performance of Daudet's *L'Arlésienne* given during the war in the famous Roman arena at Arles. It was a blazing hot day even for Provence, and the sun veering round the corner of the rickety awning must have been terribly trying to the courage of the actors and to their tempers, which showed signs of wear as the afternoon drew to evening. It was a scratch cast headed by the one-time celebrated Aimée Tessandier, an admirable actress if never quite of the highest order. Her book of recollections is full of good things. The artist relates her past with an amazing frankness, beginning with the days when as a child she was forced to pick up dung on the high-roads, and making no secret of her years of notoriety as a beauty. As an example of her wit and sincerity we may instance her own description of her efforts to acquire an American accent for the part of Julia Walker in Pailleron's *L'Age ingrat*. "Me jeter à l'eau, cela veut dire que je vais essayer l'accent. J'essaie. Ça ne vient pas. Je n'ai pas de dispositions, et pourtant je fais de mon mieux; je cours les bars; je commande des sodas, du whisky, du pale-ale, j'attrape des crampes d'estomac; je pénètre dans tous les magasins britanniques; je me ruine en objets à dénominations anglaises—je dus récemment me débarrasser d'un stock important de waterproofs acquis à cette époque—on me rencontre sur tous les champs de courses, dans des écuries, je fréquente des jockeys, des lads, est-ce que je sais? Je me fais présenter un nombre invraisemblable de misses et de mistress, j'emploie des journées entières à articuler goddam, thank you, how do you do, Washington, kiss me, cow-boy, good-night, good-bye—et cela sans prendre l'accent. Si des Americaines passent dans la rue, je me précipite, je les suis de près, je bois leurs paroles, et même, les jours de grande énergie, j'interviens dans leurs conversations. Mes amis craignent qu'à force de bonnes intentions, je ne me fasse remarquer."

But to return to *L'Arlésienne*. The scenery was of the barest description. A crazy door in the back wall would swing open now and again to reveal the Mère Renaud, a stout, red-faced woman, indulging in an after-dinner nap prior to her exquisite scene with her septuagenarian lover—an old actor who seemed a deal more intent on catching the *rapide* back to Paris than on the belated endearments of his antique mistress. A local band of enthusiasts was more than persistent in its endeavours to get the better of Bizet's immortal suite—that perfect justification of incidental music. There were numerous stage waits; the Arlesian Don José, who in the play could not be got to listen to the wooings of his Micaela, could be heard prompting her with her own proper blandishments. In the front row of the so-called balcony—the first tier of the old arena—an enormous and disconcerting negro shone and basked, and rolled under his red fez the yellow of his bilious eyes. Boys whooped and skylarked, clambering over the tiers, leaping from arch to arch, and chasing one another up and down the stone stairways. Seagulls from the Mediterranean—*mouettes* the peasant of the Midi calls them—wheeled and complained high in the blue, and once a *grand-duc* on some majestic journey paused for a contemptuous glance at the mimic scene.

It was a combination to dismay a lesser genius than Tessandier's, but this fine artist knew how to triumph over the accident of a setting and the absurdities of the Provençal stage. Up to the end of the fourth act the old lady had given a wonderful performance, full of vigour and authority. But when the players came on for the fifth act, it could be seen that she had gone to pieces. I have said that the staging was entirely inadequate. Those who have seen *L'Arlésienne* will remember the formidable staircase of the last act down which it is the tradition for the mother to tumble. It was whispered amongst the audience that the properties of the Arena did not contain a staircase. Just as well, one thought, since the old lady would be spared the physical effort. So we applauded respectfully, since the earlier acts had been magnificent, and wended our way soberly home.

I made a little détour in order to visit the ruins of the Greek Theatre on the hill; when I arrived at the hotel the artists had preceded me. In the salon I found a little, old, withered, shrunken figure. It was Tessandier, rocking herself to and fro, crying with rage. I attempted some formal complimenting, which was interrupted by a storm of protest and the unhooding of the old lady's angry eyes, the eyes of a vulture, they seemed to me.

"Non, Monsieur, ce n'était pas ça! Au contraire, j'ai très mal joué.

17

C'était vraiment trop ort. On m'avait promis le nécessaire, et vous avez vu comme ces messieurs savent tenir leur parole. Je n'avais même pas l'escalier pour le cinqième acte! C'était indigne, c'était lâche. Un moment j'eus l'idée de quitter la scène et de retourner à Paris, car je prévoyais que le dernier acte serait forcément raté et que je manquerais mon effet. Ainsi je ne fus plus maîtresse de moi-même, et j'ai très mal joué!" Then in a paroxysm of self-reproach: "Il m'a fallu manquer mon effet. J'ai du jouer au-dessous de mes forces!" To my fumbling consolation that one cannot always be at one's best, the actress replied with dignity: "A mon âge, je n'ai pas le droit de jouer au-dessous de mes forces!"

At her age! There lay the sting of the reproach. One realised that to this artist it was a tragedy to quit the scene on an anticlimax. At her age! The chance that a great career might close on a fiasco was more than she could bear.

(1917)

18

A Handful of Rogues

THE world has gone mad about bed-books; I cannot pick up a paper without seeing somebody's "best dozen". The tired brain would seem to couch best on the familiar. At least, I can find no other reason for all those Sayings of Marcus Aurelius, Snippets from George Eliot, Posies Gathered from Anna Laetitia Barbauld. For many years I have been content with three bed-books—*The Pilgrim's Progress, The Diary of a Nobody,* and *A Book of Scoundrels.* Bunyan I read at all times; the story of Mr. Pooter—"without a copy of which I regard any bedroom I occupy as unfurnished", wrote Lord Rosebery—breathing, as it does, the very spirit of Ecclesiastes, subdues me when I am overmerry; the Whibley sustains me when I am too sad. I have always adored this singer of rogues. Let those who will find comfort in Pritchard and Palmer, Cream, Crippen, and the Seddons. I mislike these pale, pestilent poisoners; they are indoor villains, exhaling the miasma of the sickroom, and their end is accomplished in a little shed. Give me Captain Hind and Sixteen-String Jack, Gentleman Harry and The Switcher. They knew the heath, the highway, and the street. Their rascality was declared, and the journey to Tyburn Tree was an honoured progress, even an apotheosis. Maidens strewed flowers in their path, and weeping doxies pinned a last nosegay in their ragged coats. "He went very decent to the gallows, with a clean napkin, and an orange in his hand", makes the most soothing of lullabies.

Some little time ago I chanced upon a treasure-trove, so that my bed-books became four. The find was nothing less than *The Pocket Newgate Calendar: A Series of Authentic Memoirs of Characters Most Famous in Their Day.* The title falls pleasantly on the ear, and you realise that these are the diaries of Somebodies, whose fame is net, clear, precise. Nor does a certain lowness, which the particular may lay to their charge, lack better sanction than mine. The Newgate Calendar kept the Bible company as the two favourite books of George Borrow! The author of my compendium is one Charles Cavendish, Esq., of the Inner Temple; its printers are Thomas Allman of Holborn Hill and William Walker of Otley. It begins, quite properly, with Jack Sheppard. If I could not have been Nelson, I swear I would have chosen to be Jack Sheppard. This captivating prison-breaker and slip-string had as much genius in his own line as Hogarth, who visited him in the condemned cell, and more than Sir James Thornhill, who would have immortalised him on canvas. "No felon ever made more noise in the world," says Cavendish with sublime simplicity, and it is a good epitaph. On the subject of Thornhill's picture, the *British Journal* bursts into poetry:

"Thornhill, 'tis thine to gild with fame
Th' obscure, and raise the humble name;
To make the form elude the grave,
And Sheppard from oblivion save.

Tho' life in vain the wretch implores,
An exile to the farthest shores;
Thy pencil brings a kind reprieve,
And bids the dying robber live.

This piece to latest times shall stand,
And show the wonders of thy hand;
Thus former masters grac'd their name,
And gave egregious robbers fame.

Appelles Alexander drew,
Cæsar is to Aurelius due;
Cromwell in Lilly's works doth shine,
And Sheppard, Thornhill, lives in thine."

Alexander, Caesar, Cromwell—this is a goodly company to join. The swelling style suits your rogue; Whibley found it impossible to explain the superiority of Rance and Gilderoy over their fellows otherwise than by parallels drawn from Euripides and the poets he overshadowed, Michaelangelo's eclipse of Donatello, the dwarfing of Keats by Shelley.

But none ever dwarfed our Jack. Once a week I make in fancy that last perilous escape, and rejoice that my guide is no bungling, second-hand reporter, but the incomparable master himself. "As my last escape from Newgate," says Jack, "out of the strong room called the Castle, has made a greater noise in the world than any other action of my life, I shall relate every minute circumstance thereof as far as I am able to remember, intending thereby to satisfy the curious, and do

20

justice to the ignorant". The last phrase is a wonderful touch. Jack could conceive acquaintance with his genius as part of the rightful heritage of mankind. Mr. Kneebone, the woollen merchant whom Sheppard had robbed, was present when the handcuffs were put on. The soft-hearted draper blubbered, and Jack had the wit to blubber, too, knowing that he could take the irons off with his teeth. But it were as well to lull his keepers to a sense of security. At three o'clock in the afternoon of Thursday, the 15th of October 1724, armed only with a crooked nail, Jack slipped his handcuffs, twisted by main strength a small piece of the chain between his legs, drew the feet-locks up to his calves and made them fast with his garters to prevent jingling. He then made a hole in the castle chimney three feet wide and six feet from the floor, and wrenched out an iron bar, two and a half feet in length and an inch square. With this he made a breach into the Red room over the castle; here he found a great nail. He then broke the door into the entry leading to the chapel. Here he was forced to break a second door and yet a third, and after that two more.

I always lose myself in the exact number of obstacles between the chapel and the leads. I imagine it was five in all. Part of the work was accomplished in the dark, and it was striking eight by St. Sepulchre's with two doors to go. Five hours' desperate work, in momentary fear of detection, his heart in his mouth, little or nothing in his belly, and only a high heart to keep him going. Once on the leads, Jack found the jump too great and was forced to go back for his blanket. Fixing this into Newgate wall with a spike which he had wrenched off in the chapel, Jack lowered himself on to the turner's leads, a house adjoining the prison. It was now nine o'clock. Fortunately the garret door was open. Down two pair of stairs the boy went, and then heard company talking in a room, the door being open. "My irons gave a small clink, which made a woman cry, 'Lord! what noise is that?' A man replied, 'Perhaps the dog or cat', and so it went off." He returned to the garret, and being terribly fatigued laid himself down for two hours. Then once more he crept down to where the company were, "and heard a gentleman taking his leave, being very importunate to be gone, saying he had disappointed some friends by not going home sooner".

What thief of our better-educated day would be able to write, or know the meaning of "importunate"? And in what follows I see a passage which bears the stamp of truth. "In about three-quarters more, the gentleman took leave and went." Jack could invent escapes; he could never have imagined those three-quarters of an hour which the gentleman occupied in getting himself out of company. The maid, who had lighted the visitor out, on returning shut the chamber door where the family was. Jack slipped downstairs, stumbled, recovered, was instantly in the entry and out at the street door, which he was so unmannerly as not to shut after him. "I was once more, contrary to my expectation, and that of all mankind, a free man."

"And that of all mankind." There speaks the artist, the incorrigible egoist persuaded that in him the world centres.

Once in the open air, our hero passed directly by St. Sepulchre's watch-house, "bidding them good morrow, it being after twelve", thence down Snowhill, up Holborn, past the watch-house at Holborn Bars, up Gray's Inn Lane into the fields, coming at two in the morning to Tottenham Court, where he slept in a cowshed. At seven on the Friday morning rain fell, and continued the whole day, so that nobody was seen in the fields. Sheppard lay snug, venturing out after dark as far as Tottenham for provisions, he having fifty shillings or so in his pockets. Friday and Saturday passed, and still Jack lay low. On Sunday afternoon the master of the shed came in, and seeing Jack's irons, asked him who he was. "I told him, 'An unfortunate young man, who had been sent to Bridewell about a bastard child, as not being able to give a security to the parish, and had made my escape.' The man replied, 'If that be the case it was a small fault indeed, for he had been guilty of the same himself formerly'; and withal said, 'However, he did not like my looks, and cared not how soon I was gone'."

Jack gave twenty of his remaining shillings to a shoemaker to rid him of his fetters, and that night came to a cellar at Charing Cross, where he refreshed himself comfortably with roast veal. Monday he sheltered in Rupert Street, and on Tuesday took lodgings in Newport market, sending for his mother and a sober, steady young woman who had for a long time been mistress of Jack's affections. And then his vanity undid him. Having successfully rifled a pawnbroker in Drury Lane, he, with part of the booty thereof, went about the town making "an extraordinary appearance, and, from a carpenter and butcher, was now transformed into a perfect gentleman". That night he drank heavily and was apprehended, scarcely knowing what was happening to him, and having but two secondhand pistols hardly worth carrying. He was executed some three weeks later, on Monday,

16th November 1724, in the twenty-third year of his age, dying "with great difficulty, and much pitied by the mob". His body was buried the same evening in St. Martin's churchyard.

It is the simplicity of this pocket edition of the *Calendar* which enchants me. "I went to work, taking off just my handcuffs," writes the boy. "No trace of the ancient slavery disgraced him save the iron anklets which clung about his legs," says the more ornate Whibley. "I was once more a free man," is Sheppard's account of his sensations on realising that he was clear of the turner's house; adding the above-mentioned pardonable allusion to the astonishment of mankind. Whereas our essayist makes him deliver his bosom thus: "Am I not the most accomplished slip-string the world has ever known? The broken wall of every round-house in town attests my bravery. Light-limbed though I be, have I not forced the impregnable castle itself? And my enemies—are they not to-day writhing in distress? The head of Blueskin, that pitiful thief, quivers in the noose; and Jonathan Wild bleeds at the throat from the dregs of a coward's courage. What a triumph shall be mine when the keeper finds the stronghold tenant-less!" Jack says simply that with part of his plunder he turned himself into a "perfect gentleman". Our essayist is more particular. "He was dressed in a superb suit of black; a diamond fawney flashed upon his finger; his light tie-periwig was worth no less than seven pounds; pistols, tortoiseshell snuff-boxes, and golden guineas jostled one another in his pockets. Thus, in brazen magnificence, etc. etc." Both ways of writing have their charm, but for me it is the felon who is the stylist. Nothing in Whibley's account can compare for dramatic tension with the hesitancies and procrastinations of the gentleman who could not take his leave. Whibley prefers the version that Jack must kick his heels upon the leads till the maid should be "silenced in sleep". It was through her "winking casement" that his road to freedom lay. Jack has nothing so ornate; his tale is of an empty garret and a party in a parlour all chattering and, we may be sure, heartily damned by the impatient youth. Yet from both narrations we get an impression of Jack's *naïveté* and something approaching lovableness. I have not read Harrison Ainsworth since I was a boy, and forget exactly how romantic he made his hero; probably he subdued the Hogarthian colouring of Jack's two doxies, Edgeworth Bess and Poll Maggot. But Ainsworth cannot have made a more seductive figure of the young man than does my pocket *Calendar*.

It is a good thing after you have sufficiently admired Constable's "Salisbury Cathedral"—which is not so much a view of that edifice as a picture of the painter as affected by spire, rainbow, foliage, pond and ducks, or whatever there may be in the foreground—it is a good thing to take a trip to Salisbury and look at the cathedral for yourself. When I was in camp at Codford St. Mary I made frequent visits to the town, and never once saw the cathedral take on Constable's mood. It is useful to have another account of Jonathan Wild and see how far that Great Man took on Fielding's mood. Fielding's portrait of Wild is monstrosity so patently idealised that we want to know exactly how big was the scoundrel upon whom the figure of the Great Man was erected. Well, this little book gives his measure. He was a great organiser—a Warwick, a Napoleon of the code, a Northcliffe. Born under other skies he would have been Pope; it is mere chance that he was Arch-prig and not Archbishop. In the commerce of our time he could have filled the shoes of Sir William Robertson or Mr. Gordon Selfridge; in the world of showmanship he would have rivalled C. B. Cochran; in that of the Hackney he might have aspired to be an Alexander Gemmell. Nature endorsed Wild with genius—and genius is genius whether in trade or deal, horse-coping or shopwalking.

The little *Calendar* does not pretend to Fielding's brilliant invention; there is nothing to match Tishy's visit to her lord on the eve of execution, desiring to ask once more: "Pray, Mr. Wild, why b—ch?" Over against this we must set the *Calendar*'s more faithful account of the laudanum which Wild took to cheat the gallows. Says Fielding: "Laudanum, therefore, being unable to stop the breath of our hero, which the fruit of hempseed, and not the spirit of poppyseed, was to overcome, he was at the usual hour attended by the proper gentleman appointed for that purpose, and acquainted that the cart was ready. On this occasion he exerted that greatness of courage which hath been so much celebrated in other heroes; and, knowing it was impossible to resist, he gravely declared he would attend them." Wild then shakes hands with those who were to conduct him to the Tree, pledges their healths in a bumper of brandy, and drives off to the acclamations of the multitude. Now consider the greater verisimilitude of the *Calendar*. "After taking the liquid laudanum, he grew so drowsy that he could not hold up his head, nor keep open his eyes at prayers. Two of his fellow prisoners, perceiving his disorder, endeavoured to rouse him. They took him by the arms and persuaded him to stand up and walk a little, which, as he was lame of the gout, he could not do without their assistance. This motion awakened him a little, and then his countenance turned very pale, he sweated violently, and grew exceedingly sick; soon after he vomited till he had thrown up the greater part of the laudanum. After this he recovered a little, but still was very drowsy, and almost insensible of what he said or did, and in this condition he was put into the cart and conveyed to Tyburn." One passage is great art; the other is truth. There is room, surely, for both.

In the case of Buckingham I want to know how Shakespeare would have a brave man die; in the matter of a malefactor, I want to know whether he possessed the one essential quality of ill doing—courage. On this point the *Calendar* is not of much help. I judge from it that Wild was perhaps not an arrant coward, but also that he was not one of the temper to spend his last earthly minute in picking a last pocket. That Wild made his entry into the next world carrying the parson's bottle-screw in his hand is a glorious flourish of a great novelist's inventive genius, but no more. Wild's execution followed within twenty-seven weeks of Sheppard's, whose glory it is that he never made friends with the thief-taker, or damned his mother's eyes.

But there are nights when I am not in the mood for Jonathan's subtleties. It is on these that I turn to the adventures of Gilbert Langley and William Gadesby. Langley, the son of a London goldsmith, was sent at the age of three to "the seat of his grandfather in Derbyshire". At seven he was "entered in the school of the Charter-house, where he soon became a tolerably good scholar". Whence we may deduce that Langley was, as they say, well connected. He appears to have led a youth of such liveliness that, in the opinion of his friends, only marriage could reclaim him. In deference to their views, he espoused a Miss Brown, a young lady whose fortune enabled him to get credit for large amounts of jewellery and cash. With these and his wife he decamped to Holland, whilst at home his creditors made him bankrupt. And now Mrs. Langley drops out of the story. Alone, her husband sails to Barbados, whence, once more head over ears in debt, he makes for Port Royal in Jamaica. There he embarks as a midshipman on board an English man-of-war, and again reaches London. Sojourns in the Poultry Compter, Newgate, and a sponging-house follow in quick succession; Langley conceives an attachment for a woman of ill fame and attempts to hang himself, but the rope breaks.

He now tries honest work as a colour-grinder, which labour so disgusts him that he contracts with the captain of a Jamaica ship, who agrees to take him to that island on the condition of selling him as a slave. Langley is, in fact, sold on arrival to a Colonel Hill, as tutor to his children. He runs away, boards a ship for England, is impressed on arrival, put on board a man-of-war, and carried round to Plymouth. He deserts, tries residence in a twopenny lodging, and again contracts with a crimp, this time to go as slave to Pennsylvania. He escapes, and we next find him at Lisbon, and after that at Malaga in Spain. Here he becomes converted to the Roman Catholic religion, enters a convent, and is recommended as a page to a Spanish lady of distinction. Follows the inevitable affair of gallantry with his mistress's niece, upon discovery of which Langley gets out of window, takes shelter with an Irish tailor, and then ship to Gibraltar. There he finds employment as waiter in the tennis court belonging to the garrison, but this does not last long. Adventures in Barbary, Santa Cruz, Oratava, Genoa, and Cadiz follow, until at length Langley finds a way to make yet another return home. In possession of a certain amount of means, he tries to find his wife, whose mother will not reveal her daughter's whereabouts. Upon this Langley "gives himself up to despair", and dissipates the whole of his fortune. Making acquaintance of one Hill, a young fellow similarly circumstanced, they agree to go to Paris, and set out to walk to Dover. An embargo being laid on all vessels in that port, they begin their return walk, and, destitute of cash, demand a man's money on the highway, and take from him the sum of three farthings.

For this they are capitally convicted, but the sentence is changed to one of transportation for seven years. Langley is transported in the month of December 1740, being still a comparatively young man, and neither the polite nor the impolite world knows him more. Through the bold outline of this story I detect, faintly, the gentleman. Many a night have I fallen asleep pondering, not on the map of Gilbert Langley's peregrinations, but of his thoughts. What were they? Had he any? Or was he a Casanova mute and unreflecting? Would he, on return from one of his farings, have been able to present a vision of anything he had beheld? I have lain awake wondering what happened to him at the end of those seven years. Perchance his fate resembled that of George Barrington, Prig of Genius, High Constable of Paramatta, and author of the immortal line: "We left our country for our country's good." Perhaps Langley also turned prig-catcher? Such an end would have been happy, characteristic, and in a double sense Gilbertian.

William Gadesby was a horse of another colour. In the minds of the unimaginative and those who know neither life nor the Sunday newspaper, Gadesby's crimes exceed probability. The narrative, says Cavendish, is taken from the condemned man's own handwriting, with corrections only of spelling and of grossly vulgar provincial idioms and expressions. J'ever see such meddlers as the tribe of Bowdler? I must now take up many hours with firking and ferreting at the British Museum and the Record Office for that which I could have read so much more conveniently and familiarly under the eider-down. I shall only glance at the story here; in the mixture of callousness and a queer sensibility its protagonist would seem to be without rival. "I was apprehended", he writes, "at Stafford for picking a man's pocket of nine guineas, and stood my trial, but did not get off without being publicly whipped." That is a good beginning. Five weeks later "I robbed a man of fifteen guineas, and stood my trial before Judge Buller, but got clear. Being too well known at Birmingham, I remained there but four weeks, during which time I drew up with a woman, and we cohabited as man and wife. I left her and took the road to Bath. I passed my time at Newmarket among the girls of the place, and for a month appeared in the habit of a gentleman, but got many a beating." Gadesby spent the following winter in Bath, having such good luck at cards that he did not need to steal except for sport. Here he became engaged to a young lady who unfortunately discovered a letter written to her lover by a crony in Exeter jail. "I then thought my character would be blasted at Bath, and I resolved to leave it; but before I did leave it, I committed the vilest action of my life, which I think the greatest sin I have to answer for to God, and for which I feel the greatest affliction. I found means to request the young lady to meet me. This she complied with. I tied my horse to the gate, and talked with her for some time; and endeavoured to reconcile matters, but to no purpose. I then treated her very ill, mounted my horse, took the road for Birmingham and never after heard of, or saw her." The blood runs cold at the thought of what a man with Gadesby's capacity for lashes would consider treating a defenceless woman "very ill".

After a period of persistent if undistinguished evildoing, Gadesby

27

enlisted in March 1784, in the 7th Royal English Fusiliers. "I joined the regiment at Gloucester, and behaved myself very well for some months." In the following February he deserted, and a few weeks later enlisted in the Dragoons, drawing three guineas bounty-money. "I joined the regiment at Stamford, and behaved myself well for some weeks." In Italy he again deserted, and got safely to Birmingham. "Having little money, I began to try my hand at thieving again. . . . Making further inquiry after my late mistress, I found she was doing extremely well. When she saw me she fainted; for, as she afterwards said, she had heard that I had been hanged at Nottingham for coining. I stopped here all night, and when in bed, she begged me to give her the history of my last travels, which I faithfully did. She pitied my situation very much, and begged me to stay with her and travel no more. I promised to do so, and next day she clothed me extremely well, and gave me a gold watch. She never wanted money, for she had then ten of the finest girls in the place in her house. I went about more like a gentleman than the bully of a bawdy-house, and was known at this time by the name of John Brown, Esq. I stayed two months with this woman, after which she was seized with a sudden fit of illness, and died. I gave her a decent burial, and ordered the girls to leave the house. I sold all the goods, and paid the landlord the house-rent, after which I had about £12."

In November Gadesby was arrested for deserting from the Fusiliers and tried by court-martial at Plymouth. "Being a likely young man, the major was not for punishing me, and I was only confined to the black hole for five days. After this I behaved myself well, and was always reckoned a good clean soldier, and gained the good opinion both of the soldiers and officers of the regiment. I took up with a woman here, and lived with her as my wife, and she kept me in pocket-money and everything I wanted."

Gadesby was then detailed for guard on board a Dutch vessel that had gone ashore, to prevent the country-people plundering her. When he was on duty he sold whatever he could of the goods under his charge, and returned to barracks the richer by twenty-four guineas and some valuables. He now persuaded his doxy to sell up her household goods and furniture. This she did, having, after all debts were paid, the sum of fourteen pounds. This kept Gadesby in drink for a considerable time, and when it was all gone he forced the woman to sell her clothes. "When I found that I had got all that she had, and there was nothing more to expect, I turned her off, when we marched from Plymouth on the twenty-fifth of April 1786." The regiment was bound for Scotland. "We arrived at Bath upon a Saturday, and were to halt all next day. In the house where I was billeted, I made a conquest of the maidservant, and we slept together. She was determined to go with me and be married, but her friends interposed. Indeed, I only intended to have carried her on as long as her money and clothes lasted."

And so the recital goes on, an interminable succession of seductions and thefts. At Dundee Gadesby was sentenced to 800 lashes for selling wearing apparel, but received only 250. This punishment did not cure him, for no sooner was he recovered than he picked a gentleman's pocket. Next he paid his addresses to a decent servant girl, who would have none of him. "It was well for her," reflects the scoundrel, "for I would have been her ruin." He goes on: "I lived, however, with another woman as my wife, and left her when the regiment marched for Fort George. I behaved myself well there for twenty weeks. But one night I went to Campbeltown, and stole some ducks, for which I received no payment but 200 lashes; and I was very ill after this punishment." In May 1786 the fellow got acquainted with Margaret Hamilton, "whom I afterwards married, and constantly adhered to since". The poor woman naturally became partner and accomplice in Gadesby's crimes, and the pair were in and out of prison with unfailing regularity, the husband returning to soldiering whenever it pleased him. In 1790, on the outbreak of war, and the regiment being ordered to Gibraltar, finding his wife would not be allowed to go with him, Gadesby deserted for the last time, and retired to Edinburgh, where he committed a series of burglaries. At midnight, on the 9th of August, a round-up by the police of all suspicious persons was carried out, and Gadesby was seized by a "very active and intelligent gentleman, belonging to the council chamber, who went out to see what was passing in the streets, till the constables should return from their duty". An accomplice turned king's evidence and Gadesby was condemned to death.

The night immediately preceding the day appointed for his execution Gadesby wrote out a confession of his being concerned in the robbery of a Dundee bank, for which two men had been already executed, and named his accomplices. This confession was handed to the Lord Provost in the morning. All the preparations for the ceremony were complete, an immense concourse of spectators was in attendance. When the hour struck Gadesby said he was ready, and wished to die. Then came a halt. Three-quarters of an hour later a respite was intimated, whereat Gadesby expressed dissatisfaction. Unable, subsequently, to pick out the people whom he had named as his accomplices, he was executed on Wednesday, the 22nd of February 1791.

An extraordinary scoundrel, and we must believe an attractive one. There is something convincing about his "I behaved myself well for such and such a period", which recurs in the narrative at least a score of times. Perhaps he was "nobody's enemy but his own"! To judge by his success with women, he must have been a fine-looking animal, and his endurance of a trifle of 250 lashes points to stamina and physique. About both Langley and Gadesby there is a certain charm; in the one case of the rolling sea, in the other of the open road. They were fresh-air fellows both, with whom you could have touched glasses. Contemplating them, the mind is not tainted with any of that queasy nonsense about the artist as poisoner. These were vital rogues, not decadent cheats.

Regretfully I pass over George Barrington, that admirable actor both of street and stage, whose performance in *The Beggar's Opera* was greatly admired; Henry Cook, who, when the warrant for his execution arrived, was so struck with the idea of his approaching fate that he "fell into convulsive fits and never afterwards recovered his health"; Captain Hind, who, knowing that within the hour his quarters would be set upon the gates of Worcester City, there to remain till they were destroyed by wind and weather, could yet make a political speech and declare his robberies to have been committed solely upon the Cromwellian faction, of whose principles he professed abhorrence.

But before my paper runs out I would, to copy Jack, satisfy the curious and do justice to the ignorant in the matter of Thurtell, Hunt, and Probert. The names read like a respectable firm of solicitors; curiously enough, whilst Thurtell was a villain, Hunt was merely weak and Probert a fool. As a boy I was familiar with an old jingle which, since I have not seen it in print for many years, I shall repeat here. It is a model of conciseness, and runs:

> "They slit his throat from ear to ear,
> His brains they battered in;

"His name was Mr. William Weare,
He came from Lyon's Inn."

It was for the murder of William Weare that John Thurtell, Joseph
Hunt, and the man Probert were indicted, almost exactly one hundred
years ago. I must ask my readers to believe that the excitement in the
little country town of Hertford on the morning of 7th January 1824
was such as Mr. James Douglas, if he had been practising at that date,
would have enthusiastically described. The plain facts of the murder
are as follows:

William Weare, addicted to play and having cheated and then
gambled one John Thurtell out of £300 at blind hookey, the latter
was determined upon revenge. On the morning of Friday, the 24th
of October 1823, Thurtell, sallying forth from the Coach and Horses
in Conduit Street, where he was in temporary concealment owing to
some undisclosed charge of misdemeanour, and accompanied by
Hunt, a public singer, visited a pawnbroker's in Marylebone and
purchased a pair of pocket-pistols. At noon Hunt hired a horse and
gig under pretence of going to Dartford in Kent, and made inquiries
as to where he could purchase a sack and a rope. He was directed to a
place over Westminster Bridge which, he was told, was on his way to
Kent. He procured these things, however, at another place, and returned to the inn in Conduit Street. There, the prosecution alleged,
Hunt was overheard to ask Probert whether he would be in at what
they, Thurtell and Hunt, were about. Counsel stated that Thurtell
drove off from the Coach and Horses between four and five o'clock,
to take up a friend, as he said to Probert, "to be killed as he travelled
with him", which expression Probert said he believed at the time to
be a piece of idle bravado. Probert's evidence elaborated all this. He
had been a spirit-dealer, he said, and rented a cottage in Gill's Hill
Lane, which left the high road to St. Albans at Radlett. The cottage
was a quarter of a mile from the high road, and fourteen miles and
a quarter from Tyburn turnpike. John Thurtell had often been down
to his cottage on sporting visits, and knew the roads and neighbourhood well. He owed Thurtell £10, and Thurtell was pressing for the
money. At the Coach and Horses on the afternoon of October 24th,
John Thurtell said to him: "I think I shall go down to your cottage
to-night. Are you going down?" He then asked him if he would drive
Hunt down. Probert said: "Yes." Thurtell said: "I expect a friend to

31

meet me this evening a little after five, and if he comes I shall go down. If I have an opportunity I mean to do him, for he is a man that has robbed me of several hundreds." Thurtell then added: "I have told Hunt where to stop. I shall want him about a mile and a half beyond Elstree. If I should not go down, give Hunt a pound." At this point Hunt came in, and Probert gave him twenty shillings. Thurtell said: "There, Joe, there's a pound; if Probert don't come, hire a horse. You know where to stop for me." Thurtell left the Coach and Horses almost immediately in a horse and chaise. It was a grey horse, and Probert believed that the horse and chaise were brought by Hunt. It was a little after five when Thurtell left.

The prosecution proved that Thurtell was seen in the course of that evening in a gig, with a horse of a very remarkable colour. He was "a sort of iron grey, with a white face and white legs—very particular marks for identity. He was first seen by a patrol near Edgware; beyond that part of the road he was seen by the landlord; but from that time of the evening, until his arrival at Probert's cottage on the same night, they had no direct evidence to trace him." The *Calendar* is a little vague here. Who is it who was seen by the patrol near Edgware—the man or the horse? Who is the landlord? Note also that there is no mention of a second party being in the gig, and we must believe that Weare was with Thurtell.

Again Probert is more particular. He says: "I afterwards set off to go in my own gig; I took Hunt with me. When I came to the middle of Oxford Street, Hunt got out of the gig to purchase a loin of pork, by my request, for supper. When we came to the top of Oxford Street, Hunt said, 'This is the place Jack is to take up his friend at.' In our way down we overtook Thurtell, about four miles from London. Hunt said to me, 'There they are; drive by, and take no notice.' He added, 'It's all right; Jack has got him.' There were two persons in the gig—Thurtell and another; I passed them and said nothing. I stopped at a public-house called the Boldfaced Stag, about seven miles from London, two miles short of Edgware. It was then, perhaps, a quarter to seven. When Hunt said, 'It's all right', I asked him what was his name? Hunt replied, 'You are not to know his name; you never saw him; you know nothing of him.' I got out at the Boldfaced Stag; I supplied the house with spirits. Hunt walked on, and said, 'I'll not go in, because I have not returned the horse-cloths I borrowed.' I stopped about twenty minutes; I then drove on, and overtook Hunt about a quarter of a mile from Edgware. I took him up, and we drove to Mr. Clarke's, at Edgware. We had a glass of brandy and water. I should think we did not stop ten minutes; we went into the bar. We stopped a little further in Edgware; and bought half a bushel of corn; I was out of corn at home; I put it in the gig. Hunt then said, 'I wonder where Thurtell is; he can't have passed us.' We then drove on to the Artichoke, kept by Mr. Field. We got there within about eight minutes of eight. Neither I nor Hunt got out. We had four or five glasses of brandy and water, waiting for the express purpose of Thurtell coming up; we thought we heard a horse and chaise, and started; I think we stopped more than three-quarters of an hour at Elstree. We went about a mile and a half to Mr. Phillimore's lodge, to wait for Thurtell. Hunt said, 'I shall wait here for John Thurtell', and he got out on the road. I drove on through Radlett, towards my own cottage; when I came near my own cottage, within about a hundred yards, I met John Thurtell; he was on foot; he says, 'Hallo, where's Hunt?' I said I had left him waiting near Phillimore's lodge for him; John Thurtell said to that, 'Oh, I don't want him now, for I have done the trick'; he said he had killed his friend that he had brought down with him; he had ridded the country of a villain, who had robbed him of three or four hundred pounds. I said, 'Good God! I hope you have not killed the man!' and he said, 'It's of no consequence to you, you don't know him, nor you never saw him; do you go back and fetch Hunt, you know best where you left him.' I returned to the place where I left Hunt, and found him near the spot where I left him. Thurtell did not go. I said to Hunt, when I took him up, 'John Thurtell is at my house—he has killed his friend'; and Hunt said, 'Thank God, I am out of it; I am glad he has done it without me; I can't think where the devil he could pass; I never saw him pass anywhere, but I'm glad I'm out of it.' He said, 'This is the place we was to have done it' (meaning near Phillimore's lodge); I asked him who the man was, and he said, 'You don't know him, and I shall not tell you'; he said it was a man that had robbed Jack of several hundred pounds, and they meant to have it back again; by that time I had reached my own house; John Thurtell stood at the gate; we drove into the yard; Hunt says, 'Thurtell, where could you pass me?' Thurtell replied, 'It don't matter where I passed you, I've done the trick—I have done it'; Thurtell said, 'What the devil did you let Probert stop drinking at his d—d public-house for, when you knew what was to be done?' Hunt said, 'I made sure you were behind or

33

else we should not have stopped'; I then took the loin of pork into the kitchen and gave it to the servant to cook for supper. I then went into the parlour and introduced Hunt to Mrs. Probert; he had never been there before."

The oftener I read this recital, the more its fascination grows upon me. (Even the muddle that much of it is has its charm.) What means did Thurtell use to induce Weare, who, conscious of the old score, must have suspected the other's enmity, to accompany him in his gig? Probably, to judge by Weare's kit, a sporting invitation. Hunt, says the prosecution, was known to Weare, but not, as he believed, "in habits of friendship". Therefore it would not appear strange to Weare that Hunt should pass him in the road without so much as raising his whip. Also Hunt was disguised by means of long, bushy whiskers. At what point in the journey did Weare first begin to suspect Thurtell's evil design? But the most curious thing about the story is the insistence with which Hunt returns to the question as to where and when Thurtell passed him, to which Thurtell will give no reply. It must, one thinks, have been either at Mr. Clarke's at Edgware, where Hunt and Probert went into the bar for nearly ten minutes, or at the corn-factor's. The point is immaterial, yet Hunt was afraid of Thurtell, and wanted to find an excuse for not having been on hand. The recital has truth stamped all over it; the touch about the borrowed horse-cloths is beyond invention.

Probert then told his wife that they were all going to Mr. Nicholson's to get leave for a day's shooting; but their real object was to go down to the place where the body of Weare was deposited. According to Probert, Thurtell carried a sack and cord, Probert a lantern. As they went along the lane Probert walked in front. Thurtell said: "Probert, he is just beyond the second turning." When they came to the second turning Thurtell said: "It's a little farther on"; and, at length: "This is the place." All three looked about for a pistol and knife, but could find neither. They got over the hedge and found the body. Thurtell searched the deceased's pockets, and found a pocket-book containing three five-pound notes, a memorandum book, and some silver. John Thurtell said: "This is all he has got; I took the watch and purse when I killed him." They then put the body into the sack head foremost; the sack came to the knees, and was tied with a cord. Then they left the body and went back to Probert's cottage. On the way Thurtell said: "When I first shot him he jumped out of the gig and ran like the devil, singing out that he would deliver all he had if I'd only spare his life. I jumped out of the gig and ran after him; I got him down, and began to cut his throat, as I thought, close to the jugular vein, but I could not stop his singing out; I then jammed the pistol into his head, I gave it a turn round, and then I knew I had done him." (The Watford surgeon called at the trial said that the wound in the temple was an inch and an eighth or a quarter in length, and seven-eighths of an inch in width. He produced the pieces of the skull which had been forced into the wound.) Thurtell then remarked to Hunt: "Joe, you ought to have been with me, for I thought at one time he would have got the better of me. These d—d pistols are like spits; they are of no use." Hunt said: "I should have thought one of those pistols would have killed him dead, but you had plenty of tools with you."

The three then returned to the house and supper. After supper Hunt sang two or three songs, Thurtell exhibited Weare's gold watch, and made Mrs. Probert a present of the gold chain. Asked where they would sleep, Thurtell and Hunt said they would share the sofa. After Mrs. Probert and her sister had retired, Thurtell gave Hunt and Probert a five-pound note and a sovereign apiece, saying: "That's your share of the blunt." They then burned Weare's books, papers and purse, and examined the contents of his carpet bag, which included wearing apparel, shooting materials, and a backgammon board containing dice and cards. During all this time Mrs. Probert was becoming uneasy. She did not go to bed, but after a time went to the window and looked out, and saw Probert, Hunt, and Thurtell in the garden. Prior to this Thurtell and Hunt had already been down to the body, but had found it too heavy to move. They returned to the cottage, and Mrs. Probert saw them take out Thurtell's horse. Thurtell and Probert went down to the land and brought the body back on the horse. Hunt took the animal to the stables and the other two dragged the body down the garden to a pond. They put stones in the sack, and threw the body into the pond. The man's feet were perhaps half a foot above the water, so Thurtell got a cord, threw it round the feet, and made Probert drag the body into the centre of the pond, where it sank. Next morning Hunt and Thurtell were out early, and some farm-hands saw them "grabbing" for something in the hedge. They explained that their gig had been nearly upset there the previous evening, and after some talk went away. The farm-hands, searching for something that they supposed might have fallen out of the gig, came upon the knife and pistol, both covered with blood.

Probert becoming nervous and insisting that the body should be removed from his pond, on the following Monday evening Thurtell and Hunt came down to the cottage. Hunt engaged Mrs. Probert in conversation, the others took the body out of the pond, put it into Thurtell's gig, and then Thurtell and Hunt drove away. They carried the body a considerable distance from Probert's cottage, and sunk it in a pond near Elstree. The murder had now become bruited about; only the body could not be found. Weare's gun, travelling-bag and back-gammon board were found at Hunt's lodgings. A penknife which was positively sworn to as having belonged to Weare was found in Thurtell's pocket, and also the fellow pistol to the one which was found on the scene of the murder. Both men were arrested, and on the strength of a half-promise by the magistrates of being admitted as an evidence, Hunt disclosed where the body was to be found.

Thurtell, at the trial, put up a most impressive defence, and rolled out his periods like a man of letters. (It is possible that Dickens used Thurtell's speech as a model for that of Sergeant Buzfuz. Dickens was twelve years old at the time of the trial, and almost certainly read the sheets of the period.) "I have been held forth to the world", said Thurtell in the best forensic manner, "as a depraved, heartless, remorse-less, prayerless villain, who had seduced my friend into a sequestered path, merely in order to despatch him into greater security—as a snake who had crept into his bosom only to strike a sure blow—as a monster who, after the perpetration of a deed from which the hardest heart recoils with horror, and at which humanity stands aghast, washed away the remembrance of my guilt in the midst of riot and debauchery." (Is not the simile of the snake in the Sergeant's best vein?)

Thurtell then goes on to flatter the jury. "You, gentlemen, must have read the details which have been daily, I may say hourly, pub-lished regarding me. It would be requiring more than the usual virtue of our nature to expect that you should entirely divest your minds of those feelings, I may say those creditable feelings, which such relations must have excited, but I am satisfied that as far as it is possible for men to enter into a grave investigation with minds unbiased, and judgments unimpaired, after the calumnies with which the public mind has been deluged—I say, I am satisfied, that with such minds and judgments, you have this day assumed your sacred office." Admirable! A kind, affectionate, and religious mother, Thurtell declared, directed the tender steps of his infancy in the paths of virtue. His rising youth was guided by a father whose piety was universally known. After leaving the paternal roof he entered the service of that later revered monarch who had been justly styled the "father of his people". He had never tarnished the lustre of his country's colours; he had fought for her, bled for her, and had not feared to shed in the open field the blood of her foes. . . . If he had been a gambler, then half the nobility in the land had been his examples, some of the most enlightened statesmen had been his companions. He bade them beware of an anticipated verdict. No man becomes wicked all at once, and therefore he should lay before them his whole career, leaving it to their clemency to supply such defects as they might observe. No pen, "though dipped in hues of heaven", could portray his feelings at this crisis. He had taken the commercial world as though it had been an army, had treated merchants as if they had been mess-companions. Naturally he became the subject of a commission in bankruptcy. He obtained the signature of all his creditors to a petition for superseding his bankruptcy. But just when he flattered himself that his ill fortune was about to close, that his blossoms were ripening, then came a frost, "a nipping frost". His chief creditor refused to sign unless he was paid a bonus of £300 beyond all the other creditors. His solicitor backed this offer, spurning which he was thrown upon the world. He had been implicated in an action for conspiracy in connection with the firing of his brother's warehouses, though the accidental nature of the combustion had been proved at a trial at which the venerable judge now present presided. . . . He trusted his language was not immoderate. But

> "The flesh will quiver where the pincers tear,
> The blood will follow where the knife is driven."

He had been charged with decoying another man to his destruction. He could prove that he was in another town at the time, but, for the sake of an amiable and innocent female who might be injured, he forbore. The Press, which ought to be the shield of public liberty, had heaped slander upon slander, and whetted the public appetite for slanders more atrocious; what in other men would serve to refute and repel the shaft of calumny was made to stain with a deeper dye the villainies ascribed to him. They, the gentlemen of the jury, had been told that after the battle he boasted of his inhumanity to a vanquished, yielding, wounded enemy, that he made a wanton sacrifice of his bleeding and supplicating foe by striking him to earth with cowardly steel, and that after this deed of blood he sat coldly down to plunder his unhappy victim. Was there an English officer, an English soldier, an Englishman whose heart would not have revolted against such baseness and folly? Had he not better fallen stemming and opposing the tide of battle upon the field of his country's glory? His particular gratitude was due to the chaplain of the prison. Let him not forget the fatherly treatment accorded him by the prison governor. His memory must perish ere he could forget such kindness; his heart must be cold ere it could cease to beat with gratitude to him, and wishes for the prosperity of his family. Here the prisoner shed tears, and the court was moved to a degree of emotion "altogether indescribable". There were no Sunday papers to describe that emotion.

Thurtell then reviewed the evidence at length, suggested that the murder was committed by Hunt and Probert, and cited a number of cases of men who had been hanged for crimes to which, afterwards, others had confessed. He implored the jury not to cut him off in the midst of his days. There was not one, he thought, in the court who did not deem him innocent of the charge. If there were, then to him or them he would say in the language of the apostle: "Would to God ye were altogether such as I am, save these bonds."

Thurtell was found guilty and sentenced to death, the execution taking place on the next day but one, the last thing he desired to know being the result of the mill between two boxers, Spring and Langham. (He made one of the party on the stage-coach with Hazlitt in the essay called *The Fight*, where he appears as "Tom Turtle, the trainer".) He was just thirty. Hunt pleaded that but for his help in the discovery of the body, there could have been no trial, and suggested that, in all fairness, so far as he was concerned, the body should be considered as undiscovered. He, too, was found guilty, and sentenced to death, but the sentence was afterwards commuted and he was sent to New South Wales for life. Probert was acquitted without giving evidence. But he did not enjoy long respite, being hanged for horse-stealing in the following year in company with two others convicted of the same crime, and a burglar. Robert Surtees witnessed the execution, an account of which was recently found among papers left by him. It concludes: "The drop suddenly fell, and a thrill ran through the crowd as those four white-covered heads assumed the same sideway attitude as they were launched into eternity."

(1924)

Sarah Bernhardt: A Postscript

THOSE who have cherished a feeling for the actor's art akin to reverence must have rubbed their eyes on seeing a whole front page of a popular newspaper devoted to the personal affairs of little Miss Mary Pickford and a bare half-dozen lines to the announcement that Madame Sarah Bernhardt had appeared in *Athalie*: "The famous actress is in her seventy-sixth year. The rôle may be described as of the recumbent order." Shudder though one may at blithe enormity, it is useless to cavil at the editorial sense of news values. To the uneducated world it really does matter what Miss Pickford eats, wears, and thinks. We were once mountebank-mad; we are now tied to the grimace. Miss Pickford is very pretty and quite a good maker of babyish faces. She brings to many "escape from their creditors and a free field for emotions they dare not indulge in real life". She gives pleasure to millions who have never heard of the great actress, or, hearing that she is an old lady of seventy-six, desire not to see her. Oh, it offends me to the soul when old age is treated so! The hey-day of a great spirit knows no passing; there is that in this old artist which shall please our children, provided they have eyes to see that which is spirit and imperishable. It were idle to pretend that the gesture is as firm, the eye as bright, the voice as liquid as once we knew them. The wonder is in the gentleness of Time, which has marred only the inessential. To him who would contribute his quota of good will this great player's art is still the quintessence of loveliness. Memory aiding, it is possible to "call back the lovely April of her prime", and looking out upon a later day to see "despite of wrinkles, this her golden time".

As the artist's physical powers have waned, so her intellectual faculties have ripened. Thirty years ago she had been content to play this foolish little Daniel with "her beauty, her grace, her flashing eye, her sinuous charm"—I quote from the catalogue of departed virtues—gathering him up to heaven at the end in her well-known cloud of fireworks. To-day Madame Bernhardt plays him, as it were, colloquially, informing unreality with a hundred little shades and accents of reality. She is fanciful, wistful, wayward, endowing little things with an actor's interest, with something of the writer's preoccupation with style. I cannot imagine any more delightful grace-note than that of the little blue flames of the rum omelette which shall enliven her loneliness. And when she quotes her line of verse you are made conscious that this is a boy's poem. She lingers over it with the tenderness of all great artists for immaturity. What panting English tragedienne, in the full measure of bodily vigour, could compass the intimacy and interest of the Frenchwoman's lowest tone and slightest motion? In the first two acts Daniel does not appear, and the stage is given over to scenes of emotion very creditably portrayed by a leading light of the *Comédie française*. We applaud, for the thing seems well done; but when, in the long colloquy with Daniel, the older artist sits motionless at her table, leaving the scene in full generosity to the younger, her very silence it is which holds us, and not the tinkle of less significant speech. What other actress, when it comes to dying, can so let life out of her voice and lineaments, so cease upon the midnight? Add to the glories of such a performance something that I would call a corona of malice, a *gouaillerie*, a Puckish hint that we shall not take this for the sublime car of tragedy, but for some workaday vehicle for tears. We are to feel that the rarer gifts of the actress have not been harnessed, and our minds are sent on haunting quest for the greatnesses that once she commanded. As a younger woman she had neither the wit nor strength of mind to make this bargain with our penetration.

A year or two ago a series of performances was announced which was to be determinate and valedictory. Equally looked forward to and dreaded, they did not, as it happened, take place. To begin with, the lady declared, in that vigorous way of hers, that the visit would in no way be one of farewell. She was not for epilogising; in any case the time was not yet. She was off to Honolulu, Hong Kong, Saskatchewan, —and merely desired to take temporary leave of the polite world. And then she became ill and the engagement was not fulfilled.

Well, there's no harm in this sort of good-bye. May this triumphant lady spend her long winter with her hand at her lips bidding adieu. That's one simile, and I would find another to fit the glory now departing. The shadows may be long; they will be longer yet before the dark, fingers to stir old memories, to set pulses beating at thought of a glamour that never was on earth. Is it our creeping age and recollection playing us tricks? Was it the artist's acting or our own youth that was the miracle? I wonder! And even as I write I know that I lie. I do not wonder. I am in no doubt.

There is nothing which does the object of panegyric so much harm as lack of discrimination in praise. Let me frankly admit that Sarah Bernhardt was never the mistress of the art of reticence, and that, great show-woman that she is, she has always turned advertisement to commodity. Take the forty-year-old history of her famous tiff with the *Comédie française*, ending in the rupture which was the necessary preliminary to those gallivantings over the unacted globe. The story of it all, so far as may be gleaned from the records of the time, is something as follows. The *Comédie* pays a visit to London, bringing in its train Mademoiselle Bernhardt, a young member whose talents have already been acclaimed by the Parisians. And here we must remember that the French, in spite of an excitable temperament, are capable of a rare level-headedness in their attitude towards artists. They know how to distinguish between the personality of the actor and his talent, and are not swayed by matters outside the theatre. "Je ne veux connaître de la Comédie française en ce feuilleton", writes Sarcey, "que ce que l'on peut en voir de sa stalle d'orchestre." The English are different. The critic of *The Times* permits himself to write: "Further, all that we have heard of Mademoiselle Sarah Bernhardt, of her various talents and manifold faculties, her character and even her eccentricities, has added to the effect produced by her acting and has made her, indisputably, the centre of our curiosity and interest in the *Comédie française*."

In the first pages of the Journal of the visit of the *Comédie* to London in 1879 Sarcey begins by deploring the coldness of the English public towards the members of the troupe other than Mademoiselle Bernhardt. He recounts for the benefit of his readers in Paris how, in spite of her altogether admirable second act in *Le Misanthrope*, Mademoiselle Croizette failed to please. How, in *Les Caprices de Marianne*, her capriciousness was ravishing, but of no avail. How, in *L'Etrangère*, the same actress displayed her greatest fascination, yet without fascinating; how, after her fine explosion in the fourth act, the audience did, after a fashion, explode in sympathy. "Mais ce n'était pas cela. Le cœur n'y était pas." The only reason he can assign is that the English cannot worship two mistresses at the same time, and that their hearts have gone out wholly to Mademoiselle Bernhardt. This is the first mention of her in the Journal and is followed by the phrase: "Oh! celle-là. . . ." "Nothing", he continues, "can convey any idea of the infatuation she has aroused. It amounts to madness. When she is about to appear a quiver runs through the audience; she appears and an Ah! of joy and rapture is heard on all sides. The house listens with rapt attention, bodies bent forward, glasses glued to their eyes; they will not lose a word, and only when she has finished break into a fury of applause. Outside the theatre they speak of no one else."

I give what happened next as related by M. Georges d'Heylli:

"It is common knowledge that this great and original artist has a distaste for behaving like the rest of the world and that discipline appears to her mechanical and wearisome. One is not mistress of several arts for nothing. Mademoiselle Sarah Bernhardt did not content herself in England with exhibiting one aspect of her charming personality: to be an actress and nothing but an actress was not enough. She established a studio for painting and sculpture where she could be admired in the delightful costume with which the photographers have made us familiar. Yielding to the numerous requests which her great talents and the general curiosity procured for her, she consented to give performances in the drawing-rooms of the aristocracy. Now, this would have been in no way the concern of either her colleagues or the Press had it not been that the stress of this additional world told so much upon the actress as to render her physically and mentally incapable of giving her best in the theatre. The day arrived when she was unable to fulfil her part in *L'Etrangère*. The bill had to be changed and the money which had been taken for the performance returned. This was followed by recriminations between the artist and the French and English Press. Mademoiselle Bernhardt, annoyed at the general censure, resigned her membership of the *Comédie française*, and accepted, or did not accept—the rumour at least was rife—an engagement for a tour in America."

Peace was, however, restored, the artist made a *sociétaire* and granted two months' holiday in the year. She resumed her performances on 17th April 1880. Shortly afterwards a critic of standing complained that she played Doña Clorinde in Augier's *L'Aventurière* in the same manner as Virginie in *L'Assommoir*.

"La nouvelle Clorinde a eu, pendant les deux derniers actes, des emportements excessifs de toute manière, d'abord parce qu'ils forçaient sa voix qui n'a de charme que dans le médium, ensuite parce qu'ils l'amenaient à des mouvements de corps et de bras qu'il serait fâcheux d'emprunter à la grande Virginie de *L'Assommoir* pour les introduire à la Comédie française."

Thus Auguste Vitu in the *Figaro*.

Sarah again resigned, and the great Sarcey was devilish cross about it. "Is it the fault of the *Comédie*", he asks, "that one of the members has preferred the rôle of star to that of artist? And then, is this so new to us Parisians? Are we not by this time used to the eccentricities of this flamboyant personage? Mademoiselle Bernhardt has resigned and is leaving us. It is unfortunate, it is true, but more particularly unfortunate for her. The *Comédie* loses a charming actress and must for the time being withdraw a few plays which are now hardly practicable without her. But the number of these plays is small, for her art, divine instrument though it be, has not many notes. Her absence is to be regretted, but we shall get over it, and another artist will arrive, perhaps Mademoiselle Bartet, who with other qualities will turn the public's head in the same way and efface the memory of her predecessor. Actors come and actors go. After Régnier, Coquelin; after Provost, Thiron; after Samson, Got; and others will succeed to the inheritance of Got, Thiron, and Coquelin. Remember the old proverb, Faute d'un moine l'abbaye ne chôme pas." Finally he delivered himself up to prophecy. "Let her make no mistake; her success will not be lasting. She is not one of those who can bear the whole brunt of a play and whose brilliance has no need of a background of mediocrity." Was ever augur more woefully mistaken? Sarcey had tried to bolster up Croizette; the world has long judged between Mademoiselle Bernhardt and Mademoiselle Bartet.

But there is another factor in this character besides wilfulness and caprice—the vacillation in artistic purpose. The Journal of the Goncourts gives a picture of her in mid-career which illustrates this. It is Edmond who writes:

10*th October*

"Lunch with Sarah Bernhardt at Bauer's, who is kindly using his influence to induce her to play my *La Faustin*.

"Sarah arrives in a pearl-grey tunic braided with gold. No diamonds except on the handle of her lorgnette. A mothlike wisp of black lace on the burning bush of her hair; beneath, the black shadow of lashes and the clear blue of her eyes. Seated at the table she complains of being little, and indeed her figure is that of the women of the Renaissance. She sits sideways, on the corner of her chair, exactly like a child who has been promoted to the big table.

"At once, with gusto, she embarks upon the history of her world scamperings. She relates how in the United States, as soon as her next tour is announced, and though it be a year beforehand, orders are sent to France for a shipload of professors in order that the young American 'miss' may know what the play is about.

"I am placed next to Sarah. She must be nearly fifty. She wears no powder and her complexion is that of a young girl. . . . She talks hygiene, morning exercises, hot baths. From this she goes on to portraits of people she has known. Dumas *fils* among others. She has a natural instinct for affability, a desire to please which is not assumed."

17*th October*

"Dinner at Sarah's to read *La Faustin*.

"The little studio where she receives is not unlike a stage setting. On the floor against the walls rows of pictures, giving the apartment something of the appearance of an auction-room; over the mantelpiece her full-length portrait by Clairin. Furniture everywhere, mediaeval chests and cabinets, an infinity of articles of virtu more or less rasta, statuettes from Chili, musical instruments from the Antipodes. Only one sign of individual taste, the skins of great polar-bears shedding a lustre on the corner where she sits. . . .

"At dinner Sarah is very gracious and full of small attentions. We return to the studio, to read the play. There is no lamp and only a few candles. The copy is typewritten and much less readable than it would have been in the usual round hand, with the result that Bauer does not read very well. The effect is cold. After the seventh scene I insist upon reading myself. I, too, do not manage very well, but I get tension into it and Sarah seems impressed by the last scene. Then tea, during which there is no further talk of the play. Finally Sarah comes over to me, says that the piece is full of passion, that the last act seems superb, and asks me to leave the script that she may go through one or two scenes which have been omitted. A few vague sentences which may mean that Sarah will accept the play, and even a phrase about putting me into touch with her manager, but nothing decisive.

"Now there are some things which are not favourable. Sarah is a romantic. At the moment the fuss they are making of Réjane inclines her towards the modern, but her artistic temperament is against it. Further, in my play La Faustin has a bitch of a sister, and it so happens that Sarah possesses one—a fact of which, until recently, I was ignorant."

44

26th November

"In reply to my letter asking for the return of my play I have to-day received a telegram from Sarah affirming a wish to act in something of mine, and asking for a further six weeks in which to think *La Faustin* over quietly. My belief is that although she may wish to give the piece she will not do so."

22nd February

"To-day without a word, the manuscript is returned."

Once free of the *Comédie*, Sarah envisages her famous world tours, and embarks upon gallivantings innumerable. And once definitely on the rampage, candour compels me to admit, as it compelled Joe Gargery, that she was indeed a buster. So began the long period of trumpeting vagabondage, and with it the history of "Sardoodledum". The actress tore about the habitable globe, piling whirlwind upon earthquake and littering the stages of half a dozen countries with the pasteboard wreckage of Fédoras, Théodoras, Toscas, Sorcières. There was probably not more than one English critic who kept his head in all this welter of popes, princes, cardinals, Russian Grand Dukes, Austrian Archdukes, German counts, cantatrices, Inquisitors, gaolers, nihilists, poisoners, and assassins. Amid the general delirium Mr. Shaw alone was heard to declare himself unimpressed by the sight of an actress "chopping a man to death with a hatchet as a preliminary to appearing as a mediaeval saint with a palm in her hand at the head of a religious procession". "Her charm", he declared, "could be imitated by a barmaid with unlimited pin-money and a row of footlights before her instead of the handles of a beer machine." Her voice he likened to the *voix celeste* stop, "which, like a sentimental New England villager with an American organ, she keeps always pulled out". But this was not criticism's general temper. Even Mr. Shaw admitted that when the actress was engaged "not in stabbing people with hat-pins, but in the normal straightforward business of acting she could do it competently enough".

There is a strange account of the actress by the Roumanian actor de Max, which the curious will not desire that I should omit:

"Il y a deux Sarah—au moins. Il y a celle qu'on voit de la salle. Et il y a celle qu'on voit des coulisses. Le malheur est que, des coulisses, on voit quelquefois la même que dans la salle, la plus belle. C'est un malheur, parce que ces jours-là, on n'est plus maître de soi; on arrive avec de la haine, de la fureur. On veut se venger d'elle, et puis on devient spectateur en jouant; quand le rideau se ferme, on lui baise les mains, avec des larmes. . . . Acteur, je connus l'actrice Sarah. Je connus aussi á son Théâtre une petite fille, qui s'appelait, par hasard, Sarah. Ai-je détesté, ai-je aimé cette insupportable petite fille? Je ne sais plus. C'est si loin. J'ai vieilli. Pas elle. C'est toujours une petite fille, une insupportable petite fille, qui a des caprices, des cris, des crises. Ah! les crises de cette petite fille!"

And yet this *petite fille* is the artist from whom "speech fell, even as her dress, in great straight folds, fringed with gold". It is the artist with the soul of Clairon's "I am eighty-five; my heart is twenty-five".

It is now twenty-two years since Madame Sarah, as she liked to be called by people who had a real affection for her, came to lunch at my mother's house at Manchester. There was much discussion, I remember, as to what ceremonies were to be observed, and what eaten and drunk. We tried to imagine what Charles Lamb would have set before Mrs. Siddons. Could we rely upon our guest "counting fish as nothing"? Our old nurse it was who clinched the matter. "I suppose the poor body eats like everyone else," she said; "her stomach will be none the worse for a good warming." There was some question as to who should hand the great lady out of her carriage and help her up the steep slope of the path. It was decided that the gardener, who for many years had performed this office for my mother, should not now be denied. If there had ever been sincerity in Adrienne's passages with the old servitor, she would, we felt, understand. You see, we were not unmindful of the fiasco of the seaport Mayor. The story goes that many years earlier the great actress was to descend upon a town which boasts of a fine council chamber, situated at the top of a flight of forty-six steps. Here, when the time came, were to be ensconced the Mayor in his robes, the town clerk, the beadle and other dignitaries. It was up these steps that the great actress was to toil. The train draws in, a state carriage with postillions and outriders is at hand. A huge crowd. A delighted Sarah sets forth, only to catch sight, after a few yards, of the stairway, at top of which, perched in his eyrie, Bumble-surrounded, awaits her the Mayor. "Ah, mais non! mais non!" she cries. "J'ai assez grimpé dans ma vie! A l'hôtel.'

Well, Madame Sarah came, and she came in state. She wore a

wonderful mantle of misty grey like the breasts of sea birds. It was in the first chill of autumn, and I like to think that the bowed trees of the garden bent still lower to touch with the tips of their branches the radiance as it passed. It was a moment or two before the presentations were over; she had brought her granddaughter and a woman friend. And then lunch, of which we could persuade our guests to touch only a quarter of a wing of chicken and some toast fingers dipped in milk. At once, to put us at our ease, she began to talk. The smallest of small talk, conventional inquiries as to what we did, a declaration that if my brothers became great men or my sister a great actress, we should not, the whole lot of us, amount to the value of our mother's little finger. About the theatre she would say very little, and it was a subject we naturally avoided. I had a feeling that one of us might suddenly, out of sheer nervousness, ask her to recite. And then, after a time, Sarah fell to talking about actors and acting, and this I take to be the finest politeness I have ever experienced. First she had some handsome things to say of English players. Of Henry Irving, whom she called a great artist and a bad actor. She admired his temperament, but his oddities, his uncouthness, his queerness of technique perplexed her, and I should certainly not have trusted her to appreciate Benson. Of Forbes-Robertson, whose Hamlet she considered a jewel to be worn on the finger of the poet himself. She talked affectionately of Coquelin, "ce bon Coquelin", and admiringly of Réjane. A very great comédienne, she called her, but rather resented my suggestion that she had great tragic gifts. "Non," she replied, "elle a la voix canaille." And then the conversation turned upon her interpretation of a part which she was then playing. This was Lucrecia Borgia, of which part I thought then, and still think, her conception wrong. Her idea of Lucrecia—and in this it must be admitted that she followed Hugo's lead—was of a perfectly good woman with a poisonous kink. She held that even if Lucrecia did entertain a passion for murder she would not show her vice except when viciously engaged. One remembered Charles Peace fiddling between thefts, but without succeeding in thinking this an apt reinforcement for her. One thought, too, of the provincial lady who was accustomed to give a lecture to schoolgirls on the occasion of the annual Shakespearian revival. Confronted with *Antony and Cleopatra*, the lecturer evaded the difficulties of her subject by announcing that she proposed to confine her considerations of the heroine's character to her aspect as a mother. This, again, did not seem a very suitable remark, and, frankly, we did not shine.

Actors are always difficult to talk to. They will not realise that all that matters is the impression the spectator actually receives, and that he is not influenced by what the actor thinks or hopes he is conveying. If only actors knew how much of the interpreting is done by the spectator and how little by themselves! We experienced, of course, extreme difficulty in putting it to Sarah that what she thought about Lucrecia was of no importance, that it was only what she made us think that mattered. In fact, we could not put it at all. We could only say that she turned Lucrecia into a good-natured goose with un-accountable moments. However, she came to the rescue with a happy "Eh bien, je vois que ça ne vous plaît pas. Qu'est-ce qui vous plaît donc?" And we tried to get her to talk about her Pelléas, which is the one perfect thing that not Mademoiselle Mars, not Mademoiselle Clairon, not ten thousand Rachels could ever have accomplished. She had singularly little to say about this, but we put it down to our not having proved ourselves worthy to be talked to. The thing we would most have instilled into her was that our admiration was critical. Youthfully we had long settled the order of her parts. First Pelléas, the butt and sea-mark of her utmost sail; then the world-wearied Phèdre; next the Jeanne d'Arc of inviolate ecstasy, and last the Marguerite, patchouli'd, but still incredibly lovely. We wanted her to realise something of this. Well, we failed. As she drove away she said something to my mother that we did not hear. The carriage receded and she waved her flowers. There was a look of grave amuse-ment in her eyes, something of the memory and the kinship of youth.

(1922)

How well I remember them, connected as they are with my first trousers. They were a beautiful pair, the material cashmere, the pattern herring-bone, the colour lavender, and, with a little black jacket, nattily filled what a photograph shows to have been a pre-possessing figure. The "cossacks", as the tailor so delightfully called them, were specially ordered to do honour to the metropolis, which I was now, for the first time, to visit. My parents had knowledge of the ways of a capital and what was due to it. My mother spoke of pictures and concerts, and my father, a good Liberal, promised me the House of Commons, and, fortune willing, a glimpse of Mr. Labouchere. But even at that early age I was all for the theatre, and my most secret wish was that I might behold Mrs. Langtry. To this end I was insistent upon being taken to Birdcage Walk. So sweet a lady, methought, should have her dovecot there.

I suppose a certain amount of pains would enable me to fix the exact year, but for tender recollections a haze is better. I remember the astonishing smartness of the hansom cabs and the silver tinkle which announced their approach in the violet summer night. The North is a land of cobblestones and rude pavings, and the rumble of a cab is heard when it is yet a mile away. But in the London of those days evening travel was silence, or something like it. Mrs. Patrick Campbell enchanting me, I must link up with the hansom drawing me to the theatre of her performance that line which she spoke more beautifully than any other Ophelia I have known:

"Like sweet bells jangled, out of tune and harsh."

I can see and hear it now—the exquisite sweep of the throat impor-tuning a happiness for ever to be denied, the wistfulness of the voice, half coo and half plaint. But Ophelia was not the first role in which I was to see this, to my young eyes, ravishing lady. Fédora with Mr. Beerbohm Tree at the Haymarket came earlier; and it was the first time that I sat in stalls having no vulgar pit, or watched the pallor of a great actress's dying come off on her lover's coat.

Women were delicious creatures then, with their leg-of-mutton sleeves, buns and monstrously absurd sailor hats. There are a hundred ways in which I can recapture the mood and spirit of the period through which they smiled and fluttered, but two generally suffice. The first is to turn to an old poem of Mr. Noyes's:

> "There's a barrel-organ carolling across a golden street
>   In the city as the sun sinks low;
> And the music's not immortal, but the world has made it sweet
>   And fulfilled it with the sunset glow."

Reading this I am a boy again, listening to *Traviata* and *Il Trovatore* as interpreted by Carl Rosa. The second way is to take down my Yellow Book. I did this yesterday, and on the random page came across the words:

> "It is easy enough to babble about the beauty of things considered apart from their meaning, to dilate on the satisfaction of art in itself, but all these phrases are merely collocations of terms, empty and meaningless. A thing can only be artistic by virtue of the idea it suggests to us; when the idea is coarse, ungainly, unspeakable, the object that suggests it is coarse, ungainly, unspeakable. . . ."

What do those sentiments here? I rubbed my eyes and read again. Yes, there was no mistake, and I can never before have read Mr. Arthur Waugh's essay on Reticence in Literature. There is a lot more about art and ethics being in indissoluble alliance, and the merits of the art being the merits of the informing idea. Now, in Nurse's phrase, did you ever? For the Yellow Book was at once the fine flower and the shrine of the perverse in art and nature. Its mission was to preach in the exquisite drawings of Beardsley the linear beauty of moral ugliness, and to inculcate in its prose such nonsense as Wilde's "The highest function of the artist is to make perceived the beauty of failure". Paradox was all the rage, and to be hailed a genius the young scribbler had but to write of the shy and bashful trumpet-orchid, or the lecherous strumpet, the common daisy. Probably the only drawing in the book of which Mr. Waugh can have approved is the immensely dull frontispiece by Leighton. But hypocrisy was ever the English way, and to preface this book of orchidacity with Leighton's Study of Two Mutes at the Funeral of Hecuba—which is not the proper title—was to ensure the patronage of Grosvenor Square. Or do I mean Kensington Gore? How otherwise to shock into buying, and propitiate into acknowledging having bought, this at the time surely outrageous publication? Its note is struck with greater honesty in the decoration to the title-page. Here we have a lady in full evening dress playing a piano in a field. There is no stool, and the musician must needs stand to her instrument. Here is declared not the immoral but the a-moral world, in which buttercups and daisies, grand pianos and grander courtesans mingle freely.

> "Then sing, ye birds, sing, sing a joyous song!
> And let the young lambs bound,
> As to the tabor's sound."

Only the bird which was to sing in Beardsley was the raven; the lamb which should bound at sight of cosmetics was the youthful Max; and the tabor to be shaken delicately and hesitantly, parenthetically and elliptically was confided to the immature Henry James. Hear the last:

"It would have been a glorious book."

"It is a glorious book," Neil Paraday murmured. "Print it as it stands —beautifully!"

"Beautifully!" I passionately promised.

So, doubtless, Messrs. Elkin Mathews and John Lane promised themselves to publish the Yellow Book. And with their consent Beardsley went on to his *Education Sentimentale*. The title is artfully stolen from Flaubert, and the drawing shows a wideawake little hussy, la Maréchale in embryo, submitting a love-letter to the surveillance of a more villainous *marchande à la toilette* than any imagined by Balzac. The next of Beardsley's illustrations is a Night Piece showing the woman whose education has been completed, perambulating and seeking, as a wit put it, the pleasure of others.

Now, I am not going to pretend that, as a boy, I derived much joy from this book. It lay on the drawing-room table, but the edict that none of us children should touch it was strict. Besides, there were better things to do then than to pore over books, yellow-covered or otherwise. Hornby and Barlow were to be admired, and many were the Saturday afternoons one spent watching the run-stealers flicker to and fro. The Dohertys were at their best, and a fellow called Vardon was doing wonderful things with a strange implement called a brassie, and there was the bicycle to master. And if one must read, were there not the school stories of Henty and Talbot Baines Reed? (Do they

51

write such ripping tales for the growing boy of to-day? I imagine that it would be a waste of time, for the wireless has abolished reading.) And for those whose tastes were older there was Stanley Weyman's *A Gentleman of France*, Rider Haggard's *Montezuma's Daughter*, and Conan Doyle's *The Refugees*. All these are to be found among the advertisements to the first number.

Yes, the Yellow Book has never for me been anything but out of date, a quaint memorial to a still quainter age. The aesthete was dead even before Shaw and Galsworthy, Wells and Bennett arose to demolish him. In his first sonnet Rupert Brooke gave forth thanks that the war had turned the youth of this country from "half-men, and their dirty songs and dreary". By which he meant, though he did not say so, all that was left in the world of the 'ninety-ish spirit.

The Japanese lanterns of Beardsley's day are all out, and the yellow of the old book has faded. Yet there are moods of nostalgia even for that which one has loved only by hearsay. Fragrance, demoded as frangipani, hangs about these old days and the leaves in which they are recorded. The gold of the 'nineties was perhaps never more than gilt, but its brief life was full of glitter. And remembering both brevity and glint, I return, from time to time, to these old-fashioned pages.

(1925)

Zola's Centenary

A HUNDRED years ago the Rue St. Joseph in Paris was, and for all I know still is, an exceedingly narrow street near the Rue Montmartre. The street was originally called the Rue du Temps Perdu, or Street of Lost Time. Before it existed the place was the graveyard in which were buried Molière and La Fontaine. After the Revolution the chapel and graveyard disappeared, and the famous bones were entrusted to a museum from which they were subsequently removed to Père Lachaise. Where there had been a graveyard, houses now arose, and in Number 10, on the 2nd of April 1840, a male child was born to a civil engineer called François Zola and his wife, Emilie. The child was given the names of Emile Edouard Charles Antoine. He was afterwards known as Emile Zola, and was to become one of France's foremost champions of liberty and her second novelist.

Where did the world of letters stand in 1840? In France, Balzac, who had still ten years to live, had successfully launched his colossal *Comédie*, Victor Hugo and Théophile Gautier were both in their full stride, and Musset was publishing his little tales in prose. The year marked a transition period. Chateaubriand, Delavigne, and de Vigny were in decline, and the young men who were to make the 'sixties and 'seventies famous were getting themselves born and educated. Stendhal in the previous year had given the world his *Chartreuse de Parme*. The elder Dumas was just beginning the full spate of his historical novels, though *The Three Musketeers* was still to come. In the year of Zola's birth, Flaubert was nineteen and had not yet written a word, just or otherwise, the Goncourts were infants, Daudet was a baby six weeks old, Anatole France had not seen the light, and Maupassant was not to begin his troubled existence till ten years afterwards.

And now to go back to little Emile. The family left Paris in 1843 and returned to Aix-en-Provence, from which François had come and where in 1847 he died. Emile was now sent to school at Aix, where his principal playmate was the painter, Cézanne. At the age of twenty Zola set out to make his own way in life, his start not being more propitious than that of Dickens in that abominable blacking factory. He grabbed at a clerkship in the Customs office in the Rue de la Douane at a salary of two francs a day, the job lasting for two months, at the end of which time he rebelled. Having found a cheap lodging for his mother, he now arranged to share a seventh-storey garret with his painter friend arriving from Aix. The pair did not remain together for very long, since young Cézanne possessed a few pence and the poet, who so far had written only a few verses à la Musset, was handicapped by a natural delicacy which prevented him from living on his friend.

Ernest Vizetelly, in a book which is still unapproached as the best biography of Zola, has this passage: "How does Zola live?—it may be asked. He himself hardly knows. Everything of the slightest value that he possesses goes to the Mont-de-Piété; he timidly borrows trifling sums of a few friends and acquaintances; he dines off a penn'orth of bread and a penn'orth of cheese, or a penn'orth of bread and a penn'orth of apples; at times he has to content himself with the bread alone. His one beverage is Adam's ale; it is only at intervals that he can afford a pipeful of tobacco; his great desire when he awakes of a morning is to procure that day, by hook or crook, the princely sum of three sous in order that he may buy a candle for his next evening's work. At times he is in despair: he is forced to commit his lines to memory during the long winter night for lack of the candle which would have enabled him to confide them to paper." In other words, Zola leads exactly the life of grim and sordid penury romanticised in Murger's *Scènes de la Vie de Bohème*.

Having nothing to eat, the young author now begins to gather material for a poetical trilogy to be entitled *Genesis*! The first part is to deal with the Birth of the World; the second, to be called "Mankind", is to be "a synthesis of universal history"; the third, with the title "The Man of the Future", is to be a masterpiece of prophecy. Zola afterwards told Maupassant that during this period he would trap sparrows at his window and roast them for food on a curtain rod! He frequently pawned his one suit and lived in nothing but a blanket, jumping into bed when any caller came. However, the end of the terrible winter of 1861 finds young Zola still alive, though of the great poem at which he has been working not more than eight lines are written.

And now things take a change for the better, an eminent medical man giving Zola an introduction to Louis Hachette, the founder of the famous publishing business. Zola starts there as a book-packer at a hundred francs a month. Obviously to the Hachette office come all the famous literary men of the period, and as young Zola is presently promoted to a clerkship it is equally obvious that, despite the shyness of its owner, that celebrated snub nose is kept busily nosing around— to receive, in its turn, nothing but snubs. But somehow or other in the year 1864 Zola's first book, the *Contes à Ninon*, is published, not by M. Hachette, but by a rival firm which gives the author no immediate payment, but is content not to exact anything for the cost of production! Here readers must be reminded that these idylls in prose are written in a strain quite the opposite of that which is to gain Zola his ultimate reputation as a realist.

For something happened which, superficially unimportant, had a determining influence on the beginner's career—young Zola's presence at the first night of the Goncourts' play, *Henriette Maréchal*. He did not foresee that the piece would occasion a storm second only to that of the first night of Hugo's *Hernani* in 1830, the occasion when Gautier wore his famous red waistcoat and Romanticism won its great victory.

"Quelle heure est-il?" somebody asks in that play, and instead of waiting to be told in the classical manner:

> "Seigneur, du haut de ma demeure
> L'horloge, enfin, sonne la douzième heure!"

is given the laconic reply: "Minuit!" The *Comédie française* had had to submit to Hugo, but that was no reason why it should give in to the Goncourts. The preface to my edition of *Henriette Maréchal* contains a note circulated to the students of the *École de Droit* which is thus worded: "Students are invited to attend the *Théâtre français* on Monday next to hiss the new play, *Henriette Maréchal*. It is imperative that this piece should not proceed beyond the first act."

The reactionaries holding that the august boards of the National Theatre could not be the home of *blague*, the piece was duly hissed off those boards, and the Goncourts' fame was made. Whereupon young Zola reflected that his *Contes à Ninon*, moderately praised by everybody, had won him no fame at all. The logic of this may have been subconscious. But the fact remains that Zola's next work of any size was that rasping study in human animality, *Thérèse Raquin*. This bringing down almost universal condemnation upon the author's head, Zola was launched, and, having in his spare time read the fifty volumes of the *Comédie Humaine*, he now conceived and proceeded to carry out the notion of a similar saga. This ultimately became the great Rougon-Macquart series—twenty huge volumes containing twelve hundred characters, and which, I confess, I am content to read as stories only.

Yet there is a great deal more to be said for these novels. Vizetelly has this: "To understand Zola aright, let us remember that he made his début at a time when science was enlarging her dominion daily. For him she exercised a fascination equal to that of art. In his youth he had turned eagerly to certain scientific studies even while he was steeping himself in poetry, and later he devoured Flourens, Zimmermann, translations of the great scientists of England and Germany. He saw that there was often a deep poetry in science; he dreamt of making it manifest—of going farther—of associating science and art, of establishing their co-relation, welding them together even in instances when to some folk they seemed to be antagonistic."

To this must be added the zeal of the reformer, about which his biographer well says: "Now, if an author desire to bring about some reformation of the community, it is natural that he should begin by portraying it. If he wish to elucidate certain social, scientific, and psychological problems for the common good, it is essential that he should in the first case state them. In that event, say some pedants, he must confine himself to treatises of the accepted form. But the author answers no, for such treatises would not reach the greater number, and his purpose would then remain unfulfilled.

"To reach them he must approach them in the only literary form for which they care; he must embody his views in novels. 'I have, in my estimation', said Zola, 'certain contributions to make to the thought of the world on certain subjects, and I have chosen the novel as the best means of communication. To tell me that I must not do so is nonsense. I claim it as my right, and who are you to gainsay it?'"

It must seem, then, that we have in Zola three men—the artist, the scientist, and the social reformer. And again I confess that it is the first which interests me most. Whatever one may think of Zola in his other aspects, there is no doubt about his tremendous power as a sheer story-teller. I know few closing scenes to equal in excitement that of *La Bête Humaine* in which the driverless and stokerless train rushes on to catastrophe with its freight of soldiers shouting: "A Berlin! à Berlin! à Berlin!" And few last words more pathetic than those at the end of *L'Assommoir*: "Fais dodo, ma belle!"

Complaint has often been made as to the ultra-realism of these novels. Of course they are ultra-real! Zola knew as well as anyone who ever lived that if you open up a dirty wound it will stink. I use this unpleasant simile because it exactly conveys the public's approach to this great writer holding the cure of public wounds to be his business. To *Germinal* he writes a prefatory note in which occurs this passage:

"I descended into the hell of Labour, and if I concealed nothing, not even the degradation of that sphere, the shameful things engendered by misery and the huddling of human beings together as if they were mere cattle, it was because I wished the picture to be complete, with all its abominations, so as to draw tears from every eye at the spectacle of such a dolorous and pariahlike existence. Those things, no doubt, are not for young girls, but family people should read me. All of you who work, read what I have written, and when you raise your voices for pity and justice my task will be accomplished."

This sympathy for the people explains why at Zola's funeral the crowd frequently broke into cries of "Germinal! Germinal!"

In 1894 came the great upheaval known as the Dreyfus Case, with which I shall not bore my readers, who ought to give me credit for this act of forbearance, since the Case is by way of being one of my pet subjects. Indeed, there hangs over my desk as I write the front page, now framed and yellowing, of that issue of *L'Aurore* in which appeared Zola's celebrated letter, "J'Accuse . . ." (It would be interesting to know how many other people possess this, either here or in France.) Zola's noble part in the Case ought to be familiar to everybody. Instead, therefore, of repeating that for which, anyhow, I have no room, I shall refer the reader to an extremely interesting chapter on Zola in George Moore's *Impressions and Opinions*, the beginning of which might easily be a parody of Moore by Sir Max Beerbohm:

"Manet had persuaded me to go to the *bal de l'Assommoir* dressed as a Parisian workman, for he enjoyed incongruities, and the blouse and the casquette, with my appearance and my accent, appealed to his imagination. 'There is no Frenchman living in London who occupies the same position as you do in Paris,' he said, and I pondered over his words as I followed him through *tout Paris* assembled at the Elysée Montmartre, for the ball given in honour of the play that was being performed at the Ambigu. 'But I must introduce you to Zola. There he is,' he said, pointing to a thickly built, massive man in evening clothes, for, as Manet said, a serious writer cannot be expected to put on fancy dress.

"Zola bowed and passed on, chilling us a little; Manet would have liked to watch him struggling into a new acquaintanceship, and we walked on together conscious of our failure, myself thinking how pleasant it would have been to have gone with them into a corner, and talked art for half an hour, 'and what a wonderful memory it would have been!' I thought, and begged Manet a few minutes later to come with me in search of Zola. But he was nowhere to be found."

Of course he wasn't! Zola knew a bore when he saw one. But Moore's essay is by no means boring.

It is, indeed, full of exciting and entertaining comment, though my real reason for referring to it is in the following remarkable coincidence. The essay concluded:

"Are we not now menaced by a novel on Lourdes, on Rome, and on Paris? In these novels Zola will rewrite everything that he has written before. His friends will drop away from him; he will be left alone; his excellent cigars will fail to attract us, and smoking bad ones in the café we shall regret his life and his works, and the mistake we made; and when the café closes we shall stand on the edge of the pavement wondering what the end will be. One of us will say, it will probably be Huysmans: 'In *Le Ventre de Paris* there is a pork butcher who, after having worked ten hours a day all his life, is found dead sitting before a table *son nez dans le boudin.*' 'And you think,' I shall say, 'that Zola will just drop from sheer exhaustion over his writing-table *son nez dans le boudin?*' "

And that, years later, is precisely what happened. Zola died on 29th September 1902, through asphyxiation by charcoal fumes from a defective chimney. He had just completed the proofs of *Vérité*, a novel about the Dreyfus Case, and had begun preparation for another novel to be called *Justice*. One is entitled, therefore, to say that he died with the famous nose glued to the last of a series of novels which, for all their undeniable flavour of black-puddings, were and have remained masterpieces.

(1940)

The Art of Gluttony

"Le pour et le contre se trouvent en chaque nation."—STERNE

NEVER do I feel my English consciousness so deeply as at the moment of quitting these shores for the entirely improbable Continent. My heart tells me that the Englishman is lord of creation, my brain argues that really I must not be such a fool. Yet it is difficult for the Englishman, who is a creature of pure sentiment, to obey the dictates of reason. Looking out of my Pullman window at high noon I behold lawn after lawn set ready for English cricket. The pitch has been rolled, our obliging English climate has done the watering, the stumps await only the bails to be imposed by umpires of an impartiality beyond the reach of foreign dagos. Here and there a flannelled figure radiant as an advertisement for Perrier water strolls about the sward making the most magnificent of imaginary off-drives. There, I say to myself, is a figure of manly sport unknown to French youth which is probably spending the afternoon with its *petite amie*.

But having made this journey a good many times I know this mood, and am always prepared to guard against it. That is why I take with me on these journeys not only our comic papers, immune alike from scandals as from humour, but one of the immortal works of Abel Hermant. "M. Hennebault était atteint d'un mal sans espoir, qui avait commencé par être insipide, mais qui avait fini par devenir sucré. Madame Hennebault ne nommait cette maladie de son mari, qui suggère des images trop inélégantes. Lorsqu'elle était contrainte d'en parler elle y substituait, par décence, une diathèse plus acceptable, et diagnostiquait l'arterio-sclérose, dont le nom double et le trait d'union lui semblaient avoir un air de noblesse bourgeoise." . . . If that sentence connecting a double-barrelled complaint with the snobbism of the double-barrelled classes does not take the reader into another world, then I am persuaded no sentence will. And as Sterne remarks, "All worlds are good". It is an instructive thing to listen to stories at the expense of one's own nationality. The following may be a chestnut, but again, some chestnuts are good. In this French gibe at English expense three milords are sitting at their club smoking their cigars. A car passes outside. "Rolls," says one. A pause. The second Englishman removes his cigar and breathes the single word "Mercédès."

Another pause, and the third club member rises and throws his cigar into the fireplace. "If you chaps are going to quarrel," he says, "I'm off." Nevertheless, though one may grant the trifle of wit, it is difficult to believe that the French have any skill in the serious business of life. One hopes that the boat will be English, the foreigner not being born who can be trusted to make any harbour less than a mile wide. And I am brought up sharp in the middle of this reflection by one with which Abel Hermant credits his delightful Madame Hennebault: "Il était moralement impossible de supposer qu'un homme si bien peigné se trompât. . . ."

I think it is the idiocy of those proceedings forcing one to fib about the number of cigars carefully wrapped up in one's pyjamas which prepares one for, and curiously reconciles one to, the larger lunacy of the Continent. After all, no statesman, no musician, no poet even, can be quite so demented as the myrmidon who defaces your luggage with little chalk crosses. By the time Abbeville is reached France has lost her power to astonish in the way of preposterousness. Just as in an asylum no act of madman is more remarkable than another, so henceforth foolishness disappears from the Continent, and the mind is prepared to accept foreign carryings-on for sober English sense. Even for something more than sense, and you begin to perceive niceties of discrimination unknown to this matter-of-fact island.

A Frenchman who had gone into the first service left on his seat opposite me a little booklet entitled *La France Gastronomique*, *Guide des Merveilles Culinaires des Bonnes Auberges Françaises*. I was inquisitive enough to make inquiry of its contents and found that it had to do entirely with eating in Paris, previous works in this series having dealt with Périgord, Anjou, Normandy, and Alsace.

The first paragraph told me that "Philippe", whose glory finally dethroned that of the famous "Rocher de Cancale", had begun its existence next door to that illustrious eating-house. Philip began life as the meanest of restaurateurs, almost a stallholder. It was genius and genius alone which enabled Philip to overcome his disdainful rival, victory dawning at the moment when he dared to replace the turbot of tradition with the innovation of "*Sole Normande*".

On the next page I beheld a portrait of Edward VII, in an irreproachable dinner jacket and his early forties, savouring the bouquet of a discreet Bordeaux. The restaurant whose glory this woodcut enhances is the Café Anglais, where Balzac laid the scene of so many famous

60

repasts. Was it not at this café that the great writer, on being presented with his bill, drew himself up to his full height with the declaration: "Monsieur, je suis Honoré de Balzac"? And the proprietor, with that respect for literature which is one of France's chiefest glories, bowed to the ground and mumbled that his kitchens and cellars were now, as always, at the disposal of so illustrious a stomach. It was at the Café Anglais that I was once sovereignly snubbed. We had had a simple dinner of four *plats*, and I noticed that in each case the waiter first put down my plate and that of my friend sitting opposite, then the dish, and that when he put the dish down it fitted to the sixteenth of an inch, though in each case it was a different size. I congratulated him upon this mechanical feat, but at once the superior fellow took the discussion into the sphere of aesthetics. "Monsieur," he said, "ou on est artiste, ou on ne l'est pas!" But even before this he had evinced signs of moral superiority. In my clumsy English way I had thought of drinking champagne, but the fellow was adamant. "Here," he said, "one drinks the Bordeaux; the champagne can be drunk elsewhere."

Who could refuse the sympathetic tear to our guide's description of the agony and passing of this sublime monument of French culture? "We think", the writer says, "with infinite melancholy of that incomparable cellar, of those macaronied chickens, of those heavenly snipe. The integrity of the proprietor of the Café Anglais was such that on the last day of its existence, when the builders had already laid pick to Gastronomy's Temple, and nothing more was to be gained from the favour of any customer, the last repast was served with the delicacy and loving attention of the restaurant at its meridian." The letterpress accompanying the woodcut of the Café's most illustrious customer is as follows: "Le futur Edouard VII fut un des meilleurs et des plus compétents clients." What race other than the French would not have wandered off into eulogies of the Prince as good son, good father, good sportsman, good diplomat, good Englishman? But no, the French author confined himself to the one point upon which, without impertinence, he might express critical opinion. Edward was a competent judge of food and drink, and the writer accepted him as an equal in a matter which knows neither prince nor commoner.

In Paris the art of famous eating is threatened. The Americans have taken it in hand, and desecration has begun. Time was when the *maître d'hôtel*, having counselled you in the choice of dishes and appropriate wines, put a screen round your table that your attention might be centred wholly and solely upon that which you had come for to eat. Other gaieties were taboo, other diners were held for a distraction. There was hush and solemnity about your table; and the first condition of existence was accorded the distinction of a rite. But the Americans have changed all that. Your sole is no longer à la Dieppoise, but à la saxophone; as you hold your melted ruby to the filtering light your view is troubled by jigging puppets who are the Western world's equivalent of the dancing Dervish; that essay in connoisseurship as to the respective merits of the Haut Brion of '93 and the La Tour of '78 is drowned in the bawl of some savage hymning "Sahara" to the maddening twang of an ill-bred ukelele. Yes, the art of delicate eating has almost died out.

Almost, but not quite. There is still Voisin, where an old-fashioned proprietor would as soon condemn his diners to the hyena's howl as to the squawk and thud of your jazz band. Voisin, with its inheritance of great claret, is another restaurant where, if you order champagne, the waiter looks down his nose. This reminds me of some lines which, by a trick of memory, have remained with me since I read them years ago. The poem—by I know not what author—was called "On Seeing Some Americans Lunching at the Carlton", and the lines run:

"Still wines within whose perfume sleeps
　　The hoarded South, they pass them by:
They like the fizzy sort that leaps,
　　Bubbles, and price, to catch the eye.

Château Larose's ruddy bloom
　　May melt the *cognoscenti*'s lip;
But has it, right across the room,
　　An air of eighteenpence a sip?"

To read Voisin's wine list, in which are included the noblest and wealthiest of the great claret growths, is to saunter on foot along the sunny slopes of fair Bordeaux.

Other places in Paris where one may still eat and drink with dignity are the restaurants patronised by the clerk and the working man. There, for the sum of four francs, you can have—and I did have—a napkin, hors-d'œuvre, a joint, one vegetable served after the joint, a fruit, cheese, and a quarter bottle of *vin ordinaire*. Coffee is extra at fifty centimes. The whole beautifully cooked, and quickly and cleanly served. Your French workman goes to his restaurant to eat, and no nigger shall order him to get up and jazz.

We English eat stupidly; the French bring to it their inexhaustible wit. I have myself seen a restaurant at the gates of a French cemetery entitled "Café du Dernier Trou". And used there not to be a little eating-house across the road from the cemetery of Père Lachaise which boasted the device: "One is better off here than opposite"? I once asked an American lady if she had visited Père Lachaise. "Only for lunch," she said, "and gee, wasn't it cute!"

In Paris a stroll to get up an appetite invariably brings us to the Madeleine, where we may, if we like, reflect upon the extraordinary genius of the French for combining the sacred with the frivolous. Was it not at the Madeleine that Bel-Ami concluded his infamous career by marrying Suzanne Walter, the daughter of his former mistress, Madame Walter? Of what does Maupassant make Bel-Ami think as he comes down the aisle with his bride on his arm? Not of Suzanne, and still less of her mother. He thinks of Madame de Marelle. The passage, which it is more proper that I should give in French, is my favourite one in all the literature of that adorable country.

"Georges descendit avec lenteur les marches du haut perron entre deux haies de spectateurs. Mais il ne les voyait point; sa pensée maintenant revenait en arrière, et devant ses yeux éblouis par l'éclatant soleil flottait l'image de Mme de Marelle rajustant en face de la glace les petits cheveux frisés de ses tempes, toujours défaits au sortir du lit."

No English writer would have dared to end a life story of five hundred and seventy-three pages with the word "bed", except, of course, in connection with repentance and demise.

"Take", says Beeton, "a dozen eggs and half a pound of butter." To which I am constrained to reply, in the words of Mrs. May: "Yes, but 'ow?" How, in these post-war days, when so many cupboards are so nearly bare, is even the most artistic of Mother Hubbards to follow the precepts of her cookery book?

A fury of impatience seizes me when I read in an expensive magazine some such paragraph as:

"I regularly model my own and Tiny's lunch—Tiny is your Daphne's ownest hubby—on 'Gourmette's' Dainty Home Menus. They are so inexpensive and no trouble to prepare. Take yesterday's:

Plovers' eggs.
Asparagus soup.
Quails.
Fraises Lenglen."

Bitterly I think of the thousands of households whose bill-of-fare is

"Bloater.
Pommes de terre Nellie Wallace.
Bread and Marg."

And then only if they are lucky!

This, I said to myself, when I opened Mrs. Pennell's new edition of
A Guide for the Greedy, is a book which I shall heartily dislike. It is an
insult to Mrs. May. Consulting it, I found, as I knew I should find,
instructions that for lunch I must first select a rare bronze from Japan,
or a fine piece of old delf, and fill it with tulips. Then I must open the
meal with salmon of a colour to enchant a Titian or a Monticelli.
Next eggs garnished with asparagus-tips are to delight me. Who, with
a soul, could pass on to a roast? asks our authoress. More to the purpose are sweetbreads, "broiled with distinction". And now a salad
"is not out of place". I am to top up with cheese—Camembert for
choice. The tulips point to claret as the wine to be drunk. "St. Estephe,
at noon, has infinite merit. . . . Coffee is to the elegantly-designed
breakfast what the Butterfly is to the Nocturne. . . . Few liqueurs
accord with it so graciously as Cognac. . . ."
And again I repeat: "Yes, but 'ow?"
And then I reflect that the book was written in 1896. It is, indeed,
part and parcel of those gracious, far-off days. The world had leisure
for nonsense then, and the money to maintain that leisure. The
working classes knew that their place was to labour cheerfully for the
non-working classes; the rich ate their bread contentedly in the sweat
of the poor man's brow. Nobody made any fuss and there was no
"social unrest". The world was just "an amusing place". There was
unemployment, perhaps, and a trifle of starvation, some overcrowding
and a fair amount of disease—rickets, consumption, fever. But since
about one per cent of the population was immune from these things
life was pronounced "amusing". "My book," says Mrs. Pennell,
"with its talk of the New Woman, of Ibsen's Nora and Hedda Gabler,

of Daudet and Tartarin, seems to date, to belong essentially to the 'nineties. That was a pleasant period for anything to belong to."

There is truth in the last sentence. The 'nineties were, indeed, a fascinating period. And, thinking of them, I surrendered to the charm of this book. For it has charm, extraordinary charm. Take that passage in praise of garlic. "Its true home is Provence. What would the land of the troubadour and the Félibre be without the *ail* that festoons every greengrocer's shop? As well rid *bouillabaisse* of its saffron as of its *ail*; as well forget the *pomme d'amour* in the sauce for macaroni, or the rosemary and the thyme on the spit with the little birds. The verse of Roumanille and Mistral swells sweet of *ail*; Tartarin and Numa Roumestan are heroes nourished upon it. It is the very essence of farandoles and ferrades, of bull-fights and water tournaments."

Here writes the true woman of letters, the artist who can transfigure the vilest material. For garlic is vile, vile beyond words. I have lived and eaten in Provence, and I know! Four unutterable, garlic-impregnated years did I spend in the neighbourhood of Marseilles. I have suffered chez Basso that abomination known as *bouillabaisse*, that stinking soup made of fish, tinctured with saffron and nauseous with garlic. But for all honest-eating Englishmen is not the condemnation of garlic already written? Does not Lucio, the fantastic of *Measure for Measure*, say of the Duke that he would eat mutton on Fridays, and worse, that he would "mouth with a beggar, though she smelt brown bread and garlic"? How often, in Provence, has not Friday brought me roast mutton stuffed with lumps of that most villainous of the onion's poor relations! How welcome in many hungry English homes were that foul dish to-day!

(1924)

"Thus to Revisit . . ."

ONE of the best traits of the Englishman is his loyalty to old favourites. If he does not wear his heart upon his sleeve, it may very well be because that rugged organ is not cut out in the accepted shape. Who would expose to view an object that is polyhedral? For I take it that that must have many sides which has many corners, and I know that the English heart has an unlimited supply of these—as many, in fact, as there are old friends to be accommodated. In this we are more generous than the French, whose appreciation of an artist, more ecstatic than ours, remains taut until it snaps, but lacks the quality of elasticity. When, as a small boy, I tried to explain to my mother how utterly beyond compare was Vesta Tilley she would smile and say: "My dear, you should have seen Judic!" Well, Judic tried to "come back" thirty years later, and the Parisians would have none of her. I cannot think but that we, in England, would have gone to meet the old artist half-way, would have covered her quavering notes with applause, and thrown, for old times' sake, a flower before her feet. In short, we should have made a better show.

Well, these old music-hall artists assembled by M. de Courville were quickly seen to be no *vieux ratés*, as our cruel neighbours put it, no "back-numbers" in our kinder phrase. Before I saw them again I had been just a little afraid that the triumph might be on this side of the curtain, in our memories only. What face should we maintain then who, when nephews have prattled to us of Billy Merson and Harry Tate, have freely admitted the excellencies of these comedians, but ended on the note of "My boy, you should have seen Arthur Roberts!" Well, now they saw him, and now they knew why, when we talk of "Arthur", there comes into our voice not only affection but a shade of that awe which genius always evokes. For genius really means the power to create, and when we behold the work of genius, be it only that of the music-hall artist, we feel in little that first wonder of Adam when he awoke to the new-made world.

The artists sat in a semicircle, with Leo Dryden as their chairman. Each performer wore a domino which, when Leo gave the signal, he or she discarded to step forth in the garb of thirty or forty years ago. The first to begin was Florrie Robina, who, in an incredibly fetching sun-bonnet, sang:

"Oh, said Aunt Matilda to her Sister Margarine."

Now, I want the reader to pause for a moment, and putting out of his mind jazz, which is not so much a rhythm as an interruption, repeat the title of Florrie's song aloud. If he does not catch the lilt the first time, let him continue until he does. How admirably, in this song, are the characters of the sisters contrasted, Matilda's sense and her flightier sister's sensibility! How perilous to the frailer Margarine would have been any prolonged stay in London; how wise, how elderly-sisterly it was of Matilda to cry "Oh!" and so home again. Charles Lee followed with some patter set to music which, even in 1888, could hardly have been called a song. But the dance which followed was very much a dance, an affair of splits and the high kick, at which we were as greatly amazed as Shallow would have been if his brother Silence had doffed his bonnet with a cavalier motion of the toe.

Then came Marguerite Corneille, singing "Hullo, Ma Baby!" with a French accent, which found Arthur irrepressible. "I say, Cornhill," he sang out, "are you any relation to Ludgate Hill?" Marguerite shrugged her pretty shoulders and reproved him in her own tongue. But whoever daunted Arthur so? He let loose a flood of verbiage composed of all the slangs—the *argot* of the quayside at Boulogne, of the guide who waylays you outside the Café de la Paix, of the promenade at the Folies Bergère, of the little tables in the cafés of the Place Blanche. He was with difficulty restored to order. "In what part of France were you born?" he was asked, to smooth matters. "Glasgow!" he replied.

Let me recall Sable Fern of the pea-jacket, trousers of white flannel, and "boater" low in the crown; Jake Friedman; Charles Bignell, whose "What Ho! She Bumps" enlivened a certain last term at school. The first note of sadness was struck by Dryden's "The Miner's Dream of Home". Leo looked as young, and, given that little forelock, as Napoleonic as ever, with a little dash, maybe, of Mr. Farquharson's Count Cenci in a cheerful moment. The singer was in full and resonant voice. Two lines of his chorus:

"I listened with joy, as I did when a boy,
   To the sound of the old village bells"

went home to every heart. The phrase is out of fashion, but I can find nothing better. And now Tom Costello and Arthur indulged in a few "words", Tom accusing his old crony of having been over a few hurdles in his time. Modestly Arthur deprecated this, admitting at most to having been "pretty good on the flat". Then Tom, with his finely featured face, tragic like Irving's, quaintly pathetic like Gerald du Maurier's, once more told us in song about going down with his ship.

It is recorded of Charles Mathews that, at an advanced age, crippled with rheumatism, he would discard stick and crutch and make entrance upon the stage in a flying leap, taking chair and table at a bound. Arthur Roberts achieved something as wonderful in the way in which he re-created the illusion of youth. When he doffed his pierrot's dressing-gown and stood forth the "masher" of the "'eighties," it was as though forty winters dropped from him. With his hooked nose and high shoulders, wide sleeves and enormous cuffs reducing arms and hands to the semblance of wings, he looked again the obscene fowl of a bygone day. This old man crumpled in his chair became young again, physically and immorally, vigorous in body and in mind, once more the hawk of the impudent promenade. He sang the unblushing days when music halls were not an alternative form of night school, with a wealth of expression, a gusto and raffishness which the present-day stage knows not, giving a perfect exposition of a lost art, of a pantomime worth whole folios of other actors' speech. With Dan Leno, Vesta Tilley, and Marie, he makes the fourth of the greatest quartet of music-hall performers the world has known. He sang a song about a lady and a bathing van. *C'est tout dire*; I, at least, shall not enlarge. In no artist now before the public can we find such vim, such fire, such force, such comic surety, such certainty of execution. Whenever, in my saunters about the pleasurable world, I encounter Roberts, I am reminded of Lamb's "Retired Leisure, to be met with in trim gardens". Perhaps it is in the vernal pleasaunce that we meet least often. Whether on some well-remembered pavement or in some beloved hostelry—where genius has a better title to its ease than idleness can ever own—wherever it be that I meet this unassuming, methodical old gentleman, I am ever impelled to make courteous salute. I refrain, but merely because I would not impose the obligation of reply.

It shall not be pretended that the eye of these old artists is as bright, the cheek as round, the step as firm as once we knew them; nor shall it be said that these things do not matter. They do matter, but least to those who see with the eye of memory; who, ageing in their turn, realise that it is the spirit and not the body which is the man. When Charles Lee, doffing his wig, reveals the meek cranium of eld, even we who are wise in these matters must refuse to believe that which our eyes have just seen.

Thomas Hardy has the lament:

> "But Time, to make me grieve,
>   Part steals, lets part abide;
> And shakes this fragile frame at eve
>   With throbbings of noon-tide."

But should not "grieve" be "glad", and is not the lament in reality a pæan? Glad must these artists be that they are enjoying that fulfilment of living and deep joy of work which exceeds all retirement, idleness and petering out soever.

(1923)

A Voyage Round My Room

Dᴏᴇꜱ anybody remember Hilary Jesson, one-time British Minister to Santa Guarda, and at all times Sir Arthur Pinero's most fatuous and, when played by Sir George Alexander, most enthralling *raisonneur*? (I like that sentence, crammed with titles fragrant of "our little parish of St. James's".) In Hilary's den at Montiago was a collection of odds and ends—"a quaint museum"—of which the best pieces were the "bloodstained handkerchief of a matador, and a cigarette, half-smoked, which has been pressed by the lips of an empress".

There are times when I fancy myself in the role of a swell-about-town, whose man gets him into a dinner jacket because he were uncomfortable else, and not because he must hie him to a playhouse and, for hire, chronicle imbecility. In these moods I look around my den in Bloomsbury and wonder which of its treasures "speak to me of friendships made all over the world". (Here Hilary would reel off half the earth's Embassies with the glibness of a waiter at a night club.) Of gallantry's trophies—the odd shoe and the gloves, "ah jamais, jamais rajeunis par les benzines", as Verlaine puts it—I possess but few, not having been a dancing man. My treasures, such as they are, speak to me not of exotic sojourns in rarefied atmospheres, but of grubbings in metropolitan holes and provincial corners. My *objets d'art et de vertu* are five—a Toby jug of George Robey with removable hat, in Doulton ware, and picked up in Long Acre; a pair of genuine Adam candlesticks in bell metal, bought in Notting Hill for the price of three articles in an always anaemic and now defunct periodical; a brass fender, formerly the property of a great sculptor and sold to me by private entreaty of his wife unbeknown to her husband, and in assuagement of an angry milk dealer; half a pair of Greek wrestlers, in papier mâché, with one toe and two fingers missing, also part of one elbow. (Or are they Roman wrestlers? Anyhow, the Embankment will know.) These, together with an ash-tray containing a cigarette, half-smoked, which has been pressed by the lips of Mr. Joseph Beckett, are all my rarities.

If I must make a *"Voyage autour de ma Chambre"*—the standby of every French writer gravelled for a theme—I think I should dwell first

70

on my pictures. I am no connoisseur, and who to me says "Norwich School" is talking gibberish. But I am persuaded that the little foreign-looking dealer who sold me that sea piece by Constable was not lying. I asked him whether this artist was at all known as a marine painter. "Not mooch," he replied, "but zat makes zis piece all ze rarer. You shall 'ave 'im at four guineas." And I had him, and he has given me as much pleasure as any authenticated canvas. I call him "Off Grimsby". Close by hangs a De Wyndt—harvesters in white smocks loading English hay against a coming thunderstorm. I went to twelve guineas for this. And for five pounds I became the owner of a view of the river above Richmond, showing a Chelsea pensioner, a sailor, and pairs of lovers dressed after the fashion of Hablot K. Browne's illustrations to David Copperfield.

Over the mantelpiece hangs a picture of Beadsman, the Derby winner of, I think, 1854. The *cognoscenti* tell me that this painting, like Gaul, is divided into three parts. They insist that the man, the horse, and the palings round the distant copse are the work of three separate artists, which, if it be true, means that I paid them a guinea apiece. The moor is a Yorkshire moor, the horse has a touch of Yorkshire blood, and the rider is pure Tyke—so much jumps to the intelligence. No southern field lies open to the heavens like those windswept acres around Pocklington and Market Weighton, neither is so much intimacy between horse and rider bred in softer shires. Next to Beadsman, a smart gig with two Yorkshire greys driven tandemwise takes the road. Three sporting dogs accompany the turnout—two at the leader's head, one behind the cart. How gay the nags look with their gamecock throats and proud heads, tails set up on their backs like aigrettes on a duchess! Well might the sale catalogue describe them as "No day too long". Are they "Safe with all road nuisances"? In their time the question was not asked. In the corner of the fireplace a tall, spare negro in pastel baffles a giant Saxon who is trying after the manner of his race to muddle through. Beneath this pair is a forgery— a print of the cricket match between Sussex and Kent, Lillywhite bowling to Fuller Pilch. The picture was painted in 1849, and the forger, clumsy fellow, has dated his print 1836!

And now I come to my most treasured possession, a prize borne off as a memento of one of the happiest evenings of my life. I had received a note from my good friend, C. B. Cochran, couched as follows:

"Dear J. A.,

"I have retrieved two bottles of tolerable champagne from my private room at the Oxford, and three of excellent Burgundy from the back of the stage at the Pavilion. A most dear lord has sent a noble haunch of venison, and I have seen something of a brace of pheasants. There is the nucleus of a feast here, after which the deluge! Will you come? Yours in all weathers.—C.B.

"PS.—I quite agree with you about B——. She kept me out of my own theatre for a fortnight."

I went, and the evening was great fun. There was a competition for whoever among the guests, including four dramatic critics, should give the name of the worst living actress, our host to judge. When the papers were opened they all contained the same name. Whereupon C.B. said severely: "How stupid you all are! Miss X—— is obviously *hors concours*." And we had to try again. The result was the young woman's mother.

After supper we fell to admiring the treasures of that charming house, and I was lucky enough to spy upon the floor, with its face to the wall, a lithograph by Picasso—"The Mountebanks." It is a study in starvation, and I took an enormous fancy to it. Then C.B. made a speech. He said: "There are two reasons why I cannot give you that lithograph. The first is that the picture is not mine, but my wife's. The second is that you, dear James, are a critic. On the other hand, I do not suppose that I shall be producing anything for at least two years, and I am certain that my wife will never forgive me if I fall below her standard in these matters. The picture is yours." And with truly Spanish generosity—for he had just returned from Spain, where, if you admire a man's hat, he will take it off and thrust it into your hands—C.B. pushed the picture under my arm. He would take none of my so feeble denials. Alas that I am now placed in the uncomfortable position of having, out of sheer impartiality, to damn his next revue! But even when I have done damning the picture will still be exquisite.

After the pictures, the photographs. I always think that a "den" should resemble as much as possible a stage-doorkeeper's cubby-hole. Of all my photographs only one is signed, and it bears in bold letters "Lily Langtry". Sarah is on the mantelpiece, wearing that mantle which I will not again describe. Next to her Réjane, toying with a little jewelled chain and looking infinitely modish. Close at hand

Ellen Terry and Forbes-Robertson in the costumes of the 'eighties peer wistfully down the years. And, even, there is a little snapshot of Henry Irving taken on the links at Cromer. He wears a broad-brimmed hat and baggy trousers, and holds a cigar in his thin hand. For once his look is less than Mephistophelian. But a mantelpiece must be more than a shrine for highfalutin' heroes and heroines, so here is Vesta Tilley celebrating some forgotten triumph—Mafeking, perhaps—and my intrepid little friend of to-day's Rodeo, Ruth Roach, looking buxom on her broncho.

This brings me to the horses, the favourites of a luckier day, whose pictures throng my walls. Let it be written of me when I die that no dramatic critic ever showed better harness ponies, nor ever exhibitor of hackneys composed better dramatic criticism. So shall I be satisfied. First there is Talke Princess, in her harness as she lived. Hers was a romantic career. Foaled in 1909, she cost 150 guineas as a two-year-old, and for three years won all before her in saddle and harness in the show-rings of Lancashire and Yorkshire. In March 1914 I sold her for 300 guineas to a banker at Lille for his daughter to drive. The little girl fell ill, and the banker wrote asking me to buy the mare back. I had filled her place and could scrape together no more than £80. I wrote the owner of this and told him how to put the mare out to grass, and how to winter her. In reply I got a cable saying that the Princess had left for England, and would I send the cheque? I went to meet her at the station on one of the last days of July, and I remember how she whinneyed with delight at almost every step of the road home. A week later the Germans entered Belgium, and a month after that Princess must go to Crewe Horse Sales, where she fetched seventy-five guineas. Mr. Henry Golding, the Liverpool magnate, bought her, selling her afterwards to the late C. F. Kenyon, the North Country racehorse owner. Princess's first foal was the world-famous Axholme Venus, unconquerable in this country when at her best, and now, alas, in America, where all our masterpieces go. Never before or since has there been such an exquisite little jewel as my Princess's daughter Venus. Tennyson has something about Maud's hand sliding out of her glove, "a treasured splendour". The simile reversed would not be nearly delicate enough for the way Venus's neck slipped into her shoulders. I was at Crewe when Mr. Kenyon, shortly before his death, put up his stud for sale. Venus was withdrawn at 3,000 guineas—a price never before asked for any harness pony. And it was at this figure that she ultimately crossed the Atlantic. But to Princess was accorded the supreme distinction of not being offered for sale at all. I make no excuse for the talk of prices. Every horse-worshipper is a dealer at heart, and price is the essence of a deal.

Next to Princess is Rusper Maryan, the three-year-old filly who won first prize for me at the London Hackney Show of 1913, at the first time of asking. It would be interesting if, in confession albums, a space were provided for "Height of Ambition". Only the actor, one thinks, would stick to his profession. In most cases the thing arrived at would doubtless be totally unconnected with the confessor's walk in life. All actors want to play Hamlet and all actresses Juliet, but I do not really believe that Mr. Pears wants to produce the best scented soap or Mr. Colgate the creamiest lather. Walter Hagen probably longs to beat Capablanca at chess, who, again, probably does not see why Mr. Gould should beat him at tennis. (No, silly, not lawn tennis!) As a small boy I wanted to score a century for Lancashire, and to this day my most dreaded nightmare is the annual match with Yorkshire at Old Trafford. We go in first and at close of play have scored 400 for six wickets, James Agate not out—o, Watson and Pilling to bat. Next morning Hornby applies the newly-invented closure, and I spend a day in the long field dropping catches.

Then came the time when I wanted to write theatre articles urbaner than Mr. Walkley's, more scintillating than Mr. Beerbohm's, soberer than William Archer's. But all these castles in Spain are but mud hovels, and the most bedraggled of chimeras. My cricket days are over. As a grown man I desire to win the harness championship at Olympia. "Wot 'opes!" as Tommy says, seeing that my stud is now one pony not twelve and a half hands high, and an unruly little handful in his leather. But when I have won that championship shall I sing a spiritless *Nunc Dimittis*? Nenni. I shall sell the victorious animal at a fabulous price, and begin all over again.

How low a thing is the theatre compared with ponies, cricket, and now golf. Closely connected with the ponies is the pet collection contained in the bag of golf clubs which stands in the corner. Years ago I was due to play in the final of a prolonged foursome tournament. My partner was a steady fellow round about scratch, and together we had to give an appalling lot of strokes to two beginners who were handicapped at twenty-four and had improved during the summer to a good fourteen. I was driving a topping little mare down to the course, and cogitating too deeply on that afternoon's match to beware of a hairpin bend in the road. Up the bank went the cart, and away went the mare, the broken shafts banging the road behind her. Fortunately my golf clubs were thrown out also. Having ascertained that no bones were broken, I left the cart—the mare was already out of sight—and scrambled over three hedges and two fields to the first tee. To cut a long story short, we halved the match, and decided on a replay on the same evening. Our opponents spent the interval in drinking weak tea and practising putting on the last green. But we were wiser, and after a steak and pint of champagne each felt like lions—at least, my partner drove like one, and his iron play was superb. Bruised and battered, I could just keep the ball out of the hazards, but once on the green I couldn't miss anything. We won by six and four, and equalled the amateur record for the course! I was sore, but the enemy were sorer. I forget how I got home. A yokel brought the mare back next day. My half of the trophy still stands on the sideboard.

(1925)

Clothes and the Player

CLOTHES have been much with me of late. But I hope not too much, as Mr. Wordsworth complained of the world in the famous sonnet! On a recent radiant morning I suddenly came upon the little Oriental gentleman who lives in the neighbourhood of Covent Garden wearing his new Chinese-red trousers which appear to be made of Christmas-cracker paper. Twirling a luminous and almost transparent greenish parasol and smoking a long cigar with unselfconscious nonchalance, he was so manifestly and completely the gentleman that nobody seemed to stare, not even the market porters.

The same night I observed supping in a famous restaurant a handsome foreign-looking young man wearing nothing but a maroon shirt, dark-blue trousers, cowhide shoes, and a girdle from which hung a dagger. When he left the restaurant he donned a magnificent blue military overcoat emblazoned with many medal ribbons, and carried in his hand a cap of white astrakhan. On inquiry I learned that he was a flying ace in the Finnish Army. And I reflect that the manners of the West End's late suppers are less good than those of the Covent Garden porters. But how blame others for staring when oneself is goggle-eyed?

It so happened that I was reading over my solitary meal Mr. Willard Connely's new biography of Beau Brummell, in which Sir Max Beerbohm is contradicted in the matter of the Beau's reason for leaving the Army. Sir Max says, in his famous essay on dandies: "One day, he rode upon parade in a pale-blue tunic with silver epaulettes. The Colonel, apologizing for the narrow system which compelled him to so painful a duty, asked him to leave the parade. The Beau saluted, trotted back to quarters and, that afternoon, sent in his papers. Henceforth he lived freely as a fop, in his maturity, should."

Mr. Connely's version is that, his regiment being quartered at Brighton, Brummell was ordered with it to Manchester to quell a riot, and that, seeking interview with the Regent, he gave Manchester as self-sufficient reason for asking permission to leave the Army. This clinched the matter, Brummell, the master courtier, adding: "Besides, sir, you would not be there!"

I wish that either Sir Max or the Beau's biographer would give us an essay on clothes and the theatre. No, I do not mean that dull thing, a history of stage costumes, but some account and explanation of how much of the fascination of playgoing is due to the clothes worn by the players. To this day I remember the magnificent effect made by Paula Tanqueray's dinner gown at Mrs. Patrick Campbell's first entry. The subject is an elaborate one, and I cannot hope to deal with much of it here. But I have often wondered whether the atmosphere of yesterday's cold mutton, which a wit once said was characteristic of all Ibsen's plays, was not entirely due to the abominable dowdiness of every one of Ibsen's heroines, excepting possibly Hedda Gabler. The fault I find with most young actresses is that instead of wearing their clothes, they allow their clothes to wear them. I suppose actresses dress principally for the woman playgoer, and take up towards males in the theatre an attitude which recalls one of my favourite passages in Henry James. The story is *An International Episode*. The Duchess of Bayswater has called on the American Mrs. Westgate, whose sister Bessie she suspects of setting her cap at her son, Lord Lambeth. And here is the passage:

" 'My son tells me you are going to Branches,' the Duchess presently resumed. 'Lord Lambeth has been so good as to ask us,' said Mrs. Westgate, who perceived that her visitor had now begun to look at her, and who had her customary happy consciousness of a distinguished appearance. The only mitigation of her felicity on this point was that, having inspected her visitor's own costume, she said to herself: 'She won't know how well I am dressed!' "

For whom, it should now be asked, do actors dress? Why is it necessary that their shoes should always be brand new, and the immaculacy of the lining in their top-hats indicate that these are being worn for the first time? Is it supposed that men care anything at all how many buttons adorn the hero's coat-sleeve, or whether the villain is bespatted or spatless? Yet there is doubtless something in the spick and spanness of a West End production, and certain stage pictures have always remained with me, of which I must be content to give two instances—one disastrous and the other delectable. The first concerns a dreadful play called *Varennes* in which Sarah Bernhardt appeared as Marie Antoinette. The scene was the inn at which the unfortunate and royal fugitives were stopped in their attempted escape, and I shall never be able to forget Sarah bewailing her fate in a horrid composition of mauve dress, puce tablecloth and auburn mop of hair. The delectable picture is that of Marie Tempest at her entry in *The Marriage of Kitty*, twirling a sunshade and then adding that lace extravaganza to the grand piano's bric-à-brac.

Since clothes have a proved effect on the playgoer, it is only reasonable to suppose that they must equally impress the filmgoer. That film managements certainly think so is proved by a large dossier just issued by Metro-Goldwyn-Mayer. This informs me that Miss Constance Cummings's fashion chart for the film of *Busman's Honeymoon* comprises a "complete answer to all queries as to what brides of the coming Season should wear for wedding and honeymoon". Here, for my women readers, is the note on the wedding dress:

"Constance Cummings chooses a gown of simple parchment satin with a train quite three yards long. A tiny waistline is achieved by scollops, which droop gently to the back, swathing the hips. The bodice is gracefully shirred and features a heart-shaped neck. The manner in which the skirt rests all the way round on the ground and the accentuated Victorian leg-of-mutton sleeves give a romantic and glamorous effect. Constance Cummings wears her hair in the loose manner which so becomes her, and the mother-of-pearl embroidered veiling and Victorian posy which she carries stress perfectly her dainty charm."

In the matter of the going-away costume, Miss Cummings is to display "an attractive suit in green tweed, with short knitted sleeves, cleverly gored skirt and matching tweed bag with tailored lime-green felt hat; the outfit is topped with a grey beaver sports coat". And so on, and so on.

My comment on all this is that the really happy bridegroom wouldn't notice whether his wife spent her wedding day getting into one marvellous confection after another or got married and went away afterwards in the old golf skirt and jumper!

Costumes seemed to me to be the whole point about the film called *Tower of London*, which is Hollywood's version of Shakespeare's *Richard III*. Every virtue of this magnificent melodrama is sedulously missed in this flat adaptation of it. Indeed, there is a consistent wrong-headedness about it which is almost winning! Gloucester, for example, has hardly any hump and looks as handsome and elegant as Mr. Basil Rathbone can make him. The worn-out Edward IV is played by Mr. Ian Hunter in full pride of health and spirits, while Mr. Vincent Price as Clarence is not allowed to impart any of the false and fleeting quality and is condemned to be pure oaf. Will it be believed that there is no mention of the Duke of Buckingham in the film? If there is, it must be merely in passing, and I certainly did not hear it.

On the other hand, I freely admit that the scene of the drowning of Clarence is magnificently done, and so is everything that leads up to the episode. And there is a grand Bosworth Field at the end which is composed like a series of battle pieces by Rubens. But all of this is negatived by the choice of Mr. Boris Karloff in the wholly subsidiary part of the Public Executioner, now swollen to Gilbert and Sullivan proportions. Mr. Karloff's performance is an excellent simulation of ogredom, but it has overtones from other films which prove fatal. The result on the night I attended was a continuous ripple of laughter.

The whole thing augurs badly for Hollywood's newly-mooted proposal to film Shakespeare's major tragedies, beginning with *Hamlet*. This would be all right if Hollywood would bear in mind the one cheap, essential thing in connection with any filming of Shakespeare— the proper speaking of the words. Get this right, and the more that is spent on the expensive inessentials such as costumes and battle shots the better. Get it wrong and all Hollywood's carpenters cannot excuse the project or justify it.

Miss Gertrude Kingston has chosen to begin a strong-minded book of reminiscences with the statement: "I have always been wanting in the intrinsic gift of success." If this is so—and Miss Kingston should be the best judge—it can only be because of her super-intellectuality. She shows in her book, *Curtsey While You're Thinking*, a perfect knowledge of French, German, and Italian. She paints serious pictures, confesses to translating the plays of Pirandello for fun, and admits to years of activity as a political speaker.

Now, the British public's notion of an actress is somebody whom you can pat on the shoulder and call a little dear. With this modification that in the case of a great actress you call her a great dear. This book justifies anybody who has always felt that patting Miss Kingston would be like patting one of the lions in Trafalgar Square. It contains no idle gossip, no frivolous stories, nothing about love or scandal, and nothing about clothes. Indeed, clothes are a sore point with our author. Miss Kingston so terrified the dramatists in whose plays she acted that not daring to praise the beauty of her acting they would descant upon the merit of her clothes: "Bernard Shaw in some early theatrical criticisms had even referred to me as 'that genius in dress', and nothing offended me more—whenever quoted by those who thought it a compliment—than this damning by faint praise of an actress in mentioning the 'cut of her jib'. As well write of a young statesman praising the becoming angle at which he wears his hat when he is out to save his country. . . ."

But Henry Arthur Jones, who was a much greater wit than people have ever given him credit for, knew how to combat this delicious Tartar. He wrote:

"DEAR GERTRUDE KINGSTON,

"I own up. I don't know anything about clothes, but you have always given me the impression of being a well-dressed woman. I dare say I was mistaken. Please forgive me. You can't deny you acted splendidly in my plays. Don't tell me I am mistaken in this. Well, never mind about your clothes. . . . You and I should make one great effort to save the country. When shall we begin?

"Always yours,
"HENRY ARTHUR JONES."

There are two stings in this charming communication. "I dare say I was mistaken" is obvious. The point about "saving the country" is that at the very moment Miss Kingston was in full electioneering blast, and that Jones knew it!

Many old and beloved names run through this book, all of them with the writer's kindly yet astringent comment. It was to Ellen Terry that Miss Kingston went to ask advice how to get on the stage, and in the glow of that remembered sun all this writer's asperity vanishes:

"Ellen received me with all the glamour of her charm in which her genius consisted. Hers was not of the same order as the sex attraction to which I alluded earlier, but an enveloping net of enchantment that she flung over man, woman, and child alike, over all those who saw, heard or spoke to her. She seemed to have sprung from the 'mythic turfs where danced the nymphs' that Botticelli might have transcribed to canvas had he been a pagan! Of course, she held up her hands with a lively gesture of horror when I told her I wanted to go on the stage, and of course she did her duty when she counselled me to 'stop off and go on painting'. I argued that I had more liking for the theatre than the studio. She very caustically observed (for she had a nice sense of

umour) 'that the people who loved acting were frequently without
alent for it'. "

Towards the end there is an astonishing record of a spirit conversation with Oscar Wilde. Here is Miss Kingston's account of how it was
set in motion:

"Becoming interested in this shadow on the blind, this outline of an
old friend without a presence, I begged the medium to give me a
séance at my house. She very kindly accepted my invitation, and after
dinner we adjourned to my workroom on the second floor, above the
disturbance of street traffic; seated by her side while my left hand
rested on the arm that held the pencil, my right hand withdrew the
sheets of paper rapidly, when covered with her writing. Meanwhile,
we talked on other topics as the pencil, once started, flew over the
pages, and until there was a pause at the end of a paragraph we did not
interrupt nor read what had been transcribed."

Then follows the writing of the automatic pencil, which appears
to have dealt in third-rate *Dorian Gray* and whatever the medium
subconsciously recollected of the Wildean wit. I have no criticism to
offer of this, having an entirely open mind on the subject of spiri-
tualistic séances. But I know that Wilde in his lifetime never wrote or
spoke trash of this order:

"Publicity is the soul of success. Nothing succeeds without the
glaring light of the sun fixed on it, and by the sun, of course, I mean
the fixed star that reigns supreme in Fleet Street! Immensely it would
revive me. I should breathe again as I did in July, when I felt like a fish
which had risen to the surface for a moment. I am quite prepared to
rise again."

On the other hand, there is something of Oscar in this:

"Ask Gertrude to speak to me directly. In past days, when beauty
still reigned in the theatre, she upheld the banner not only of beauty,
but of the more severe virgin, intellect."

And something, too, in this sentence:

"I have ventured in this play" (there was question of a three-act play
said to have been received by the automatic medium) "to place before

the public a hope, so I call that third act of mine, a 'hope that somethin
awaits them after death that savours less of the graveyard and tha
unutterably inartistic receptacle, the coffin, than of the upper air'."

Yes, but, dear Miss Kingston, don't you realise that if Oscar ha
written that he would have shortened it? Oscar knew not only a
about wit, but all about polishing, and if the sentence is genuine Wild
it only shows that the next world is a great impoverisher of style. An
why, dearest Miss Kingston, did you not include in your book a hal
or even a quarter of a scene of something alleged to be Wilde's play
so that we could judge for ourselves of its authenticity?

(1937)

Ypres in Retrospect

⁌⁍⁌⁍⁌⁍⁌⁍⁌⁍⁌⁍⁌⁍⁌⁍⁌⁍⁌⁍⁌⁍⁌⁍⁌⁍⁌⁍⁌⁍⁌⁍

ᴌᴇᴛ not my title deceive the reader. I was never in Flanders before 4th August of last year, and until that day knew Ypres only in the spirit. I do not presume to write here for those who remember the little town in the time which was at once its agony and its hey-day; it is not for me to go fumbling among sacred emotions. For sacred they must be, whatever cloak the Englishman may use to make them presentable before his shy soul.

I write rather for those who have known that which was once called the Salient by hearsay only and at second-hand, from the dispatches and newspaper reports. Second-hand, yet it is to be thought that, in those days, knowledge came to us in some way which was not a mere piecing together; we saw Ypres in a flash. Imagination is the lightning of the mind, and the murdered landscape, for those who knew it not, became in those years of battle suddenly familiar as the fields of boyhood.

Everything was exactly as I expected to find it—in the spirit. Superficially, all was changed. Belgium is healed. Every wound is closed and every shell-hole is filled up; those fields to-day are as fair as our own. True that the forest of Houthoulst still stands in naked distress, its ruined choirs remaining for a token and a memory. Six miles of Ostend there rises from the smiling land a fragment of what was once a château, striking upon the eye with all the suddenness of a *coup de théâtre*. For the rest there is not more desolation than you shall see in the old football ground at Stamford Bridge. Nature has forgiven.

It is impossible to believe that War was ever here. Even the old bricks are cleared away, and those heaps of smoking ruins are once again a village. There is, perhaps, a trifle too much ecstasy of new red brick, and a smack of unreality about these pink houses with the terra-cotta roofs; they are overflushed with victory.

Soon after passing the ruined château the chauffeur stopped and pointed to a flourishing farmhouse. It was there, he said, that ten of his regiment were surprised by the Germans. Six of his comrades were killed; he and three others escaped by hiding themselves in straw. A plain fairy tale; there never was any war! At Dixmude they gave us beer in a little café called *A la bataille de l'Yser*, but still it was as though peace had always reigned. The bridge over the canal is not yet completely repaired, but the interruption of the traffic does not seem of greater significance than Piccadilly knows. Dixmude was beflagged, one guessed in some purely civilian celebration.

Shortly after leaving this prosperous village we saw the first of the monuments, that erected to Guynemer by his brother airmen. This is essentially French in its exquisiteness of form, and also, be it said, in the unashamed rhetoric, almost the theatricality, of its inscription. At the top of a tall and elegant column is a flying stork, neck and legs outstretched, supported, one gathers, by the dropped wings. On the plinth is a bronze inscription which Cyrano de Bergerac might have devised, acclaiming Guynemer as individual hero—"Héros légendaire tombé en plein ciel de gloire"—but also presenting him as symbol of the qualities of the French race and an example "meet for the noblest emulations". But in reading this rhapsody you forget the humble dead and remember Corneille.

A mile or so farther on stands another monument. From a granite sheath grow the head and shoulders of a Canadian soldier. The head, crowned with the familiar helmet, is bent, the hands are folded upon a reversed rifle; the soldier watches over those who sleep beneath. On the front of the plinth is the single word "Canada". On the sides, in raised yet hardly decipherable lettering, is the bare statement:

"On this spot 18,000 Canadians on the British left withstood the first German gas attack, April 22-24, 1915. 2,000 fell and were buried here."

This has almost the power of the Greek: "Stranger, depart and tell the Lacedemonians that we lie here obeying their laws." One bows the head, in humble acceptance; the bravest ornament were out of place. There is a mysterious power in this brooding figure, drawing you from the things that are to the things that were. It does more than command the landscape—it orders the spirit. The Guynemer monument is a pretty thing and a fine gesture; this is the soul of those who fell. It is conceivable that a grey day might add to the spiritual significance of this memorial; in the blazing August sun its shock is overwhelming.

Not far away is the "Oxford Road" Cemetery, containing the bodies of those who fell here, 1915-1918. This quiet acre is beautifully kept. A little wooden shrine by the simple entrance-gate contains the roll of those whose names are known. It is unlocked, so that we who pass may read.

The first of the tiny tombstones is to one unnamed. It bears at the top the words "A Soldier of the Great War", and at the bottom, "Known unto God". The second marks the resting-place of an unnamed Australian soldier, known unto God. The third gives the name of an English boy, his drummer's rank, his regiment and regimental device. And so on. These are the poet's rich dead, who

> "Laid the world away; poured out the red
> Sweet wine of youth; gave up the years to be
> Of work and joy, and that unhoped serene
> That men call age."

It is these graves which bind up the England that is with the England that was, which bring back the exaltation and the catch at the throat, that sense of the fullness of life which leapt singing into the arms of Death. Just as some jolly boy gave the name of "Skindles" to the little *estaminet* which is now the biggest hotel in Ypres, so his "Oxford Road" fancy is to be preserved for ever.

On this bright August day the years fade, and here again are the wind and the rain, the mud and the engines of terror, the unending boredom and the swift pain. Once more English humour and our land's imperishable spirit walk the earth. These things, having once been, must ever be. But you have to stand before these simple stones to realise that, in essence, England has not changed, and that at heart we have not forgotten.

And now the journey takes on the aspect of a dispatch from the front. Poelcappelle, Langemarck, St. Julien, Zonnebeke—the names of these hamlets bring back old amazement.

At last we spy the tower of the Cloth Hall, from which a flag is flying. As we approach, the sound of the hurdy-gurdy strikes upon our ears; there is a fair in full swing. There, in that market-place once swept by mortal hail, at the very feet of the hallowed pile on the spot where our dearest fell, are the steamboats and the roundabouts. One's first thought is that this is the very abomination of desecration. And then one reflects that the war was fought that peaceable citizens the world over might enjoy their fairs in peace. For hundreds of years, perhaps, at this season and in this place there has been gaiety; we conquered that this should still be. The dead will understand. Still, it is something of a shock that, as we turn into the Menin Road, the car should be held up by competitors in a cycle race. For if anywhere there be sacred ground, it is surely here. There are sideshows now, and a booth in front of which women are dancing . . .

The road is smooth to-day and we bowl along at a fair pace. Hooge has its brand-new château, and Sanctuary Wood is a pleasant coppice. At the memorial erected to the Gloucesters just before Gheluvelt I stop and ponder upon those tiny prominences, Passchendaele, Hill 60. Once they were the boundaries of the civilised world.

We return via Poperinghe and Furnes, and at Nieuport cross the Yser, which, with its bridge, is exactly like the photographs. And then home. Strange that in a few short hours you can turn a page of history which four years wrote in the blood of a generation! Strange how the world has shrunk! Strange that there can be such a thing as dressing for dinner in this land of the mighty dead! But the clock goes on, and life must be lived. The dead hear no human sound, no click of gaming counters. But for myself, I forsake the saloons, watch the sun go down into the sea, and sit staring at vacancy till the stars swing to their places.

(1924)

On Looking into "Little Arthur"

∽∽∽∽∽∽∽∽∽∽∽∽∽∽∽∽∽∽∽∽∽∽∽∽∽∽∽

It was the extraordinary success of *Oliver Cromwell* at His Majesty's
Theatre which prompted me to look again into my first history book
—*Little Arthur's History of England*. There are certain things which,
while memory holds, I know that I shall never forget. They are the
eleven inseparable prefixes to German verbs, the dates of the first four
"proper" English kings—one doesn't really count those Saxon fellows
—and, for some curious reason, the unique export of Greece. Often I
wake up in the middle of the night repeating "Be-emp-er-, ent-ver-
zer, etc.", or "William I, 1066; William II, 1087", and so on; or I cry
out aloud: "The principal export of this country is currants."

Three names there are in English history which I shall never forget,
and they are not to be found in any list of our Great Men. Yet they
stand out more clearly in my mind than Simon de Montfort, Wat Tyler,
or Perkin Warbeck. They are the names of Dr. Juxon, Mr. Herbert,
and Colonel Hacker. The first was Bishop of London, the second a
valet, the third a soldier of sorts. This is an odd trick of the mind which
needs no Freud to elucidate. The explanation is simply that two of
these were impressed upon my childish brain as the names of the most
faithful friends of the unhappiest monarch in history. To their lasting
shame neither Wills, that late lamented dramatist, nor the present
distinguished Mr. Drinkwater have made mention in their dramas of
these two noble people. It was Lady Callcott who, in *Little Arthur*,
immortalised them.

I could have repeated with perfect accuracy, any time during the
past thirty-five years, this, to me, most purple passage in all literature:

"The next morning, very early, the king called Mr. Herbert to help
him dress, and said it was like a second marriage day, and he wished to
be well dressed, for before night he hoped to be in Heaven. While he
was dressing he said: 'Death is not terrible to me! I bless God that I am
prepared.' Good Bishop Juxon then came and prayed with Charles,
till Colonel Hacker, who had the care of the king, came to call them.
Then the king walked to Whitehall, and as he went one soldier prayed,
'God bless him.' And so he passed to the banqueting house, in front
of which a scaffold was built. King Charles was brought out upon it,

and after speaking a short time to his friends and to good Bishop Juxon, he knelt down and laid his head upon the block, and a man in a mask cut off his head with one stroke."

As a child I was as much a sentimentalist as the grown-up Mr. Chesterton. I naturally preferred cricket or even trap-and-ball to history lessons, yet confess that on wet days I often read certain parts of *Little Arthur* for sheer amusement. They were chiefly the accounts of the Spanish Armada, Gunpowder Plot, and this most romantic and dastardly execution. There was a spot of iron-mould on the page, and in some childish way I got it into my head that this was a drop of the royal martyr's blood, spilled by that deft and single blow. I have never been able to see how any well-brought-up child could be other than a Royalist.

Listen to our authoress on the Protector:

"This Cromwell was a Puritan, or Roundhead. He was brave and very sagacious, and very strictly religious according to his own notions, though some men thought him a hypocrite; at all events, he was always thinking how he could make himself the greatest man in England."

And I am not at all sure that even Mr. Drinkwater's imaginary portrait gives me any very different notion.

I remain as much a Royalist as I was at the age of ten. The best picture of Charles is not Van Dyck's, but *Arthur's* little woodcut which shows him in the act of handing to the good Bishop his Order of the George set with diamonds, prior to laying his head on the block. I looked into the book yesterday for the first time since childhood, and was surprised to find how greatly in this picture Charles has come to resemble Sir Thomas Beecham.

I spent the whole day in reading this really wonderful little book. England is described as "joined to another country called Scotland, and the two together are called Great Britain". What have little Welsh boys to say to this slight? Of Ireland I read:

"It was never conquered by the Romans; and the people were as ignorant as the Britons before the Romans came, with just the same sort of houses and clothes. They might have been in the same state for many years if a very good man, whom the Irish called Saint Patrick, had not gone from Britain to Ireland and taught the people to be Christians; and he and some of his companions also taught them to read; *and the Irish people began to be a little more like those in other parts of the world.*"

There is an admirable sanity about our historian, and her insistence upon the peculiar magnanimity of the English in victory links the days of St. Athelstane with those of the Boer War. There is one passage concerning the nobility which I would have written in letters of gold over the cot of every little budding Bolshevik. It runs:

"Now, when a man has been made a noble, and his name is remembered because he is good, or manly, or clever, or brave, or wise, his sons will say to themselves, 'Our dear father has been made a noble because he was good or brave; we must be good or brave or useful, too, that people may see that he taught us well, and that we know how to love and honour him by following his good example.' . . . The nobles of England are useful to the country. As they are rich enough to live without working for themselves and their families, they have time to be always ready when the king wants advice; or when there is a Parliament to make laws; or when the king wishes to send messages to other kings. And as their forefathers were made noble because of their goodness, wisdom or bravery, they have in general followed their example, and they have always, next after the king, been the people we have loved best, and who have done us the most good."

And then follows a passage which makes me wonder whether the dear lady had not her tongue at times ever so little, delicately and deliciously, in her cheek.

"When you are older you will understand this better, and you will find out many more reasons to be glad that we have noblemen in our own dear country."

Two chapters have been added since I was a boy:

"King Edward's reign, though short, was a time of many changes. One of the most remarkable movements was the demand of women for votes. Now, I should like you to understand that a great many wise people were in favour of this, but, unhappily, the more violent agitators amongst the women, by breaking windows and setting fire to houses, so put the people against it that any chance it ever had of being passed was extinguished."

Little Arthur is a delightful book. Peruse it again, dear reader. Perhaps, like me, you will find many things that you have forgotten. Perhaps, again like me, you will wonder how Queen Elfrida's servant, shown in the picture as standing at the off shoulder of an earlier King Edward's horse and facing that thirsty monarch, contrived as the king was drinking to stab him in the back. The text stipulates this, however, and if you see a thing in *Little Arthur*, it is so.

(1924)

De Senectute

~~~~~~

THERE are two subjects—Death and Old Age—upon which our essayists write an intolerable deal of rubbish. *Pace* Plato, Cicero, and all the ancient crowd whose names end in that doleful vowel, and asking pardon of old fogies such as Bacon and Montaigne, there is nothing favourable to be said of either that ultimate or penultimate condition towards which all mankind moves at a gallop. Old Age makes one of Shakespeare's joyless catalogue; its fellows are gout, serpigo, and rheum. "Be absolute for death" is nonsense; and nonsense, too, is the craving for eld.

The best that can be said for Old Age is that it is an unendurable state which old men manage, somehow or other, to endure. And endure with considerable equanimity, courage, and even hope. That Old Age should hope seems to me to be the triumph and vindication of the spirit of man. It is a thousand times more significant than the despair of youth, puling romantically for a grave too far away. During the war I came across a remarkable instance of the hopefulness of Old Age. I am, perhaps, betraying no grave military secret when I say that my duty during that stirring time was to keep the horses of our Near Eastern Army supplied with fodder. There is not a hayfield in sleepy Provence which I did not come to know like the back of my hand, whilst at one time I could reel off the names of all the railway stations between Marseilles and Salonica with fewer mistakes than, as a boy, I could recite the table of the Kings of England. I once calculated that the hay trucks which I dispatched during those four years would, placed end to end, have reached from London to Manchester and back again to Crewe. But that is by the way.

One day when I was sitting in my office in Arles, whose life has not changed since through its streets Hannibal marched his Numidians to the sack of Italy, whose women trace their beauty to Phoenician sailors —one day an old, old man creaked himself with difficulty into my room, and, taking off his hat with a gesture magnificent despite its decrepitude, said:

"Sir, you are the first English officer I have had the pleasure of addressing since Sebastopol."

The old gentleman was the last flowering of one of the ancient families of France. He was a bachelor, and the title would die with him. On his breast he wore two medals—one of which had been awarded him for services during the Crimean War, in which he served as sub-lieutenant.

"And the other?" I asked.

"I was in charge of the first balloon which was sent up from Paris during the siege of 1870," he replied.

I tried my hand at a compliment.

"You have served your country, *mon capitaine*," I hazarded.

"*Commandant!*" he said sharply. He had come to haggle about the price of his last year's hay crop carefully garnered against a rise, and was full of hope about the crop now growing and of complaint that he had been forced to postpone the building of a new house, upon which he had set his heart, until after the war.

"Après la guerre finie," I murmured, in my best soldier-French. "Roll on, peace!"

"Nous les aurons!" he said simply. "And then I shall build my new house."

Afterwards he went on to tell me of a new conservatory, and a wonderful system of heating of his own invention.

"If that succeeds, I shall, etc. etc. . . ."

I remember some ten years ago taking tea with an old lady aged eighty-five who lived in the New Cut. She boasted—if that is the right word—of having lived in the same house for thirty-seven years, of having entered no place where intoxicating liquor is sold for forty-six years, of being the eldest and last surviving member of a family of eleven, the baby of which family, her youngest brother, she buried at the trifling age of sixty-three. My friend remembered the return of her cousins—two privates and a captain—from the Crimea in 1855 better than the return of her neighbour's sons from France in 1919. She was proud of her uncles who fought at Waterloo. But she was prouder still that when she died there would be enough to bury her. What was over was to go to a great-grandnephew, whom I invariably found playing in the gutter and whose curls were a golden dream in a dull street. For him my old lady laid "monstrous foundations". For him she was flushed with hope.

Shakespeare enumerates amongst the good things which may accompany Old Age, "honour, love, obedience, troops of friends". I cannot say to what extent these privileges were enjoyed by M. le

Commandante, le Comte de X——. That old French nobleman struck me, for all his gallantry, as a wintry personage, frosty, and not too kindly. But then I only met him in my official capacity. Whereas I know that the way of life of my old friend of the New Cut had fallen into the sear, the yellow leaf, with all imaginable gentleness. She was honoured by the neighbourhood and had troops of friends, among whom I was proud to count myself. She had all the love that four-year-old little Charlie could spare from grubbing in the gutter. Whether she had his obedience is another matter.

I often wonder what the end of life must be like for those poor folk who have nothing to look back upon save an infinity of steps washed, floors scrubbed, beds made, and rooms "turned out". Perhaps theirs is the peace which còmes with mere cessation from labour. Perhaps, like the old man in the story, sometimes they sit and think and sometimes they just sit. Perhaps with them Old Age is just an endless Saturday afternoon.

It is always something of a shock when an elderly acquaintance makes disclosure of two parents, or even of one. Some time ago I spent a week with an old friend, well on the shady side of sixty, who unaccountably slipped away every evening for the hour between nine o'clock and ten. Curiosity getting the better of manners, I asked my friend what was the cause of his absence. He told me, with a somewhat shamefaced air, that his father had been blind and bedridden for the past five years, and that every evening, whatever he was doing, he gave up an hour to the old gentleman, and to reading aloud the novels of Walter Scott. The extent of this filial devotion can only be measured when I say that my friend is an amateur, almost to frenzy, of Meredith, James, and even later schools of English letters. Scott bores him to tears. The picture of an old man approaching his ninetieth year, blind, bedridden, and dependent upon a son for one hour's daily relief from ennui—this picture gives one to think. Yet it may be that, even at ninety, all is not darkness and tedium, that adventures of the spirit remain.

I remember another son who was in the habit of taking his father, a distinguished man of letters, well over ninety, for a drive in a victoria every Saturday afternoon. On one occasion I accompanied them. The old gentleman appeared to both of us to be very, very old, harder of hearing than usual, and also, it seemed, harder of understanding. For a time my friend babbled the small talk which he deemed best suited to his father's declining intelligence. Suddenly the old man roused himself, shot a glance of scorn, and said:

"Arthur, you talk like a fool! If you have nothing intelligent to say, then say nothing!"

Will the reader forgive another personal experience? I am privileged to retain the friendship of my father's oldest friend, a singer and singing master of great renown, whose name is world-famous. The maestro is eighty-eight, brisk, hale and hearty. We were in a bus recently, into which clambered, with infinite difficulty, a rheumatic stripling of not more than seventy. My companion laughed his jovial roar, like a lion well pleased, shook a white mane, and in a voice loud enough to be heard of the whole company, said:

"It must be a terrible thing to grow old!"

My old friend and his doctor are, for the moment, not on the best of terms, the latter having incautiously suggested that at eighty-eight it were a reasonable thing to give up bicycling! This medical man should have been philosopher enough to know that to him who loves life more than he fears death it is never the time to give up anything, and that reason does not enter into the matter.

Some time before Sarah Bernhardt died I remember reading a newspaper paragraph to the effect that the great actress had expressed her intention of appearing during the following season, if she had her health, in a play by Sacha Guitry. That paragraphist lied! What Sarah said was that she would appear *whether she had her health or not*.

I see in all these instances the flame of indomitable courage in the face of Old Age.

> "With wrinckled wimpled forehead let old yeares,
> While we may, be resolv'd to merrie cheere,"

writes old Montaigne, echoing still older Horace. This is the courage which makes a Goethe begin the conquest of a new language at the age of eighty, which sends a Johnson in his sixty-fifth year a-touring in the Hebrides. Stevenson tells us that it is better to lose health like a spendthrift than to waste it like a miser. The precept applies even more forcibly to our declining years. "By all means begin your folio; even if the doctor does not give you a year, even if he hesitates about a month, make one brave push and see what can be accomplished in a week. It is not only in finished undertakings that we ought to honour

94

useful labour. A spirit goes out of the man who means execution which outlives the most untimely ending." And the most timely ending, too. That's my whole point. If I were a great novelist who had completed my hundredth year and written my hundredth book, I should, praying God, set out cheerfully on my hundredth and first in both kinds. What says the preacher? "In the morning sow thy seed, and in the evening withhold not thine hand; for thou knowest not whether shall prosper, either this or that, or whether they both shall be alike good."

Vaguely I remember at school poring over a Latin writer who babbled of Old Age. Cicero was the fellow's name, and the whole class thought him rather tosh. But then we didn't believe in the subject; Old Age seemed a long way off. And now it is here. Or very nearly here. I am going to tell you how I know.

When I was a small boy of six the great event of the year was a holiday by the sea. I can remember the feel and smell, almost the taste, of the red plush lining to the yellow cab which bore us to the station, the excitement which went to the bagging of a window-seat in the train, the ecstatic moving off, the feverish counting of the stations, the mystery of the luncheon basket, the rapture of arrival. I remember the path up to the front door of the lodgings, the hydrangeas in the front garden, the bow-window, the broad smile and bosom, the Welsh welcome of Mrs. Evan Williams. I remember the taste of the butter, the odour and feel of the sheets, the way the little lattice window of my bedroom opened on to Puffin Island and the sea.

And then there was the beach. The first thing was to ascertain about the tides—i.e. the hours at which cricket on the sands would be possible, and the last moment for completing one's castle. The next was to renew old acquaintance with the owners of fishing-smacks, and glean news of the shrimping prospects. But I need not go on. You, reader, have launched boats with golden keels and mother-of-pearl sails into seas of tumbling sapphire and diamond spray. You, too, have chased little crabs, wept over a dead starfish, pondered upon the infinite beauty of the common shell, gazed fearfully upon the tribe of Coelenterata, Medusae, and hydroids as they floated singingly by. Perhaps you have known the horrible delight of vivisecting a jellyfish with a spade! Of a surety you have gazed with rapture upon those Sixth Form heroes sporting incredible blazers, impeccably creased flannels, and boots of an immaculate, dazzling white. Like me, you have thought on the day when you would be able to hit a full-pitch for six beyond the jetty. Like me, you have known contempt for those old gentlemen lolling in the shade of a boat, with their backs to the sea and their bespectacled noses in the financial column of *The Times*. You, too, have known pity for those half-hearted fellows who were obviously afraid to face fast bowling, and would slink away to knock silly little balls into silly little holes on some waste ground remote from the sea. Weakling, craven-spirited folk these! One decided that they must be old.

Last week a friend blew in and proposed that I should run down with him to the East Coast. He was feeling off-colour, and told me that I was looking jaded. Great Yarmouth was his suggestion. "If you like," I yawningly assented. "All those places are the same." We got uninterestingly to Liverpool Street, and chose seats in the train with less regard to the view than to the absence of the draught. We toyed with a five-course lunch, and played piquet. As for counting the stations, I can only say that I do not know whether we went via Cambridge or Ipswich, or both. We spent an hour or so deciding upon our hotel. After dinner my friend went off to a picture-palace to see Nazimova in *Salome*. I made inquiries about the golf courses in the neighbourhood, wrote some letters, and went to bed early. I have to confess that throughout the whole of that week I did not once put my foot upon the seashore. Not a toe and not a finger did I dip into that uncomfortable, unnecessary sea. Not a castle did I construct. What a waste of land for building sites! Once, whilst I was sitting on a cheerless form on the front trying to discover what Ooboolulu Tea and Rubber Estates had done during the previous week, a cricket ball hit me full in the chest, and I heard a shrill voice crying: "That's four! The old bloke counts as a boundary!" I confess that I found myself thinking that there is a proper place for cricket, and that that place is not the seashore. . . .

I had some very enjoyable games of golf, principally with the local professional, who conceded me six bisques without difficulty. Once I found the very top of my form, and, getting round in seventy-four, or one under par, beat the pro. And now I know that I am getting old. I shall probably never beat a professional golfer again, and I know that it really won't matter if I don't. Whereas, when I was the age of the small boy who counts old gentlemen as boundaries, it mattered enormously whether I made twenty runs or only nineteen. But it will matter tremendously what Ooboolulu does in the way of rise or fall. Yes, I am old. . . .

Lest the reader be too greatly depressed, let me declare that most of the foregoing is a lie. It is true that I went to Yarmouth and played one magnificent round. But it is untrue that I care anything at all about Ooboolulu shares. I haven't got any, and they can go to £1,000 or drop to 9d. for all I care. What happened when the kid hit me was that I joined the game, bowled him and his side out, and scored forty-six off my own bat, *all run*.

(1924)

To Quote or not to Quote

My Christmas presents this year consisted of two hyacinths, six pocket handkerchiefs, and a little book entitled *Common Misquotations*, by Hesketh Pearson. Each of us, I suppose, has his favourite misquotation, being the trap he digs for himself. Mine is the line in *Macbeth*:

> "Look like the innocent flower
> But be the serpent under't."

This is said not, as you might naturally suppose, by Macbeth to his lady, but by the wife to the husband. Nevertheless, I am always tempted to use it the other way round. Some little time ago there was a discussion in one of our Sunday papers as to the origin of a passage nowhere to be found in Shakespeare:

> " 'Tis now the very witching hour of night,
> When churchyards yawn, and graves give forth
> their dead."

Hamlet's words stop at "yawn", the rest of the passage being:

> "and hell itself breathes out
> Contagion to this world."

Some held that the misquotation arose from following the logic of the passage too closely. If and when a churchyard yawns, what can it do except disgorge its occupants? Others held that Barry Sullivan was responsible for an emendation which he thought an improvement, and one critic produced evidence that that great and robustious actor always garbled the passage so. A simpler explanation is that whoever the actor was had running in his head Calpurnia's warning to Caesar:

> "A lioness hath whelped in the streets;
> And graves have yawned, and yielded up their
> dead."

Mr. Pearson omits the most common of all Shakespearian misquotations: "The play's the thing." As normally used this can only mean that nothing matters except the play. But Hamlet does not stop when

98

his followers do. He declares that the play's the thing wherein he'll catch the king's conscience. Only in that sense does it matter at all.

The reason I always verify my quotations is, first, a passion for accuracy, and, second, that you never know. I suppose the most familiar line in English dramatic poetry is the first line of Hamlet's soliloquy in Act III. This is his third soliloquy, not counting the "Remember thee!" speech addressed to the vanished ghost. Every reader knows the speech I mean, and has quoted its first line when about to take some plunge. But will you, reader, swear that you know whether there is, or is not, a comma after the first "To be"? Try this on your literary friends, and at the same time ask them to fill in the missing adjective in the lines from Gray's *Elegy*:

> "Along the cool, sequestered vale of life
> They kept the —— tenor of their way."

It's a safe bet that they will say "even". But the tongue was ever an unruly member, which phrase is not to be found in the Scriptures, the nearest passage being: "But the tongue can no man tame; it is an unruly evil" (General Epistle of James iii, 8). I suppose in this case the mind harks back to the Belly and Members parable. Or am I thinking of a Fable by Æsop? The tongue is also often an untidy member at the service of a slovenly mind. This is the reason for the imbecile if generally accepted couplet:

> "A man convinced against his will
> Will hold the same opinion still."

The actual lines in *Hudibras* are:

> "He that complies against his will
> Is of his own opinion still."

Or is it that the ear is out of control? Suppose I write: "Every highbrow who has no other claim to distinction grows a beard." It is ten to one that somebody will quote me as having said: "No man with a beard has any claim to distinction." Darwin is always supposed to have based his theory that Man was descended from Monkey on the statement that formerly Man had a tail. What Darwin said, always presuming it was not Lamarck, was that some monkeys have no tails. Montague, who was a master of the art, said that his difficulty was a photographic memory, which enabled him to see with his mind's eye the words on the page and the stops as well. To give his "quotes" an air of naturalness he would change an unimportant word, and mis-quote on purpose! That, I think, is a virtue, or at least a sign of extra-ordinary literary sensitiveness. A vice in quotation is to go to your bookshelf for a handful of saws and instances and write your article round them; I know one eminent journalist who, before he begins an article, has five minutes' rummaging in a Dickens concordance.

But taste, it seems to me, is changing, and the appetite for quotation is not what it was. To-day we are impatient of what was formerly a passion in the author and a delight in the reader. Montaigne has a passage about filching authors who, "amidst their trivial compositions, intermingle and wrest in whole sentences taken from ancient authors, supposing by such filching-theft to purchase honour and reputation in themselves, doe cleave contrarie. For this infinite variety and dissem-blance of lustres makes a face so wan, so ill-favored and so uglie, in respect of theirs, that they lose much more than they gaine thereby." Yet Montaigne was a famous quoter. No essayist ever quoted more extensively or unblushingly; at a moderate estimate one may put Montaigne's borrowings at one-tenth of his total matter. Bacon in his "essays" has one hundred and thirty-one quotations from the Latin alone. Burton's *Anatomy of Melancholy?* This is all plums and no pudding.

To-day's feeling is all against the critic who lards his prose with the fat of other men. I think that in this the reader is wrong. A good writer quotes not to embellish his own matter, but to enrich his reader's mind. Nor does he quote because he is in a hurry, though a modern marshaller of other men's riches has given us this gem: "Originality is the thief of time." The conscientious quoter does so because he has something vital to say, something he is not going to be prevented from saying, and which has already been said in words better than any he can himself invent. I find that in *Sesame and Lilies* Ruskin quotes the Bible fifty-two times, not, I think anybody will say, out of vanity or haste. Take that passage in which he analyses the character of Achilles in the great Homeric story:

"Intense alike in love and in friendship, he loses, first his mistress, and then his friend; for the sake of the one, he surrenders to death the armies of his own land; for the sake of the other he surrenders all. Will a man lay down his life for his friend? Yea—even for his *dead* friend, this Achilles, though goddess-born and goddess-taught, gives up his kingdom, his country, and his life—casts alike the innocent and guilty, with himself into one gulf of slaughter, and dies at last by the hand of the basest of his adversaries." (By a lucky miracle—unless the sage of Coniston arranged for it in his proofs—the words "Will a man lay down his life for his friend?" exactly fill one line, and with enormous effect.) Will the reader ask himself whether Ruskin, great master of prose though he was, could have found ten words which would have been an improvement on St. John's?

(1934)

One Circus for the Rich

~~~~~~

> "Try I will; no harm in trying:
> Wonder 'tis how little mirth
> Keeps the bones of man from lying
> On the bed of earth."
>
> A. E. HOUSMAN,
> *A Shropshire Lad*

PROMISE a child that you will take him to see equestrians and a clown and he will set up, says Mr. Kenneth Grahame, a rhythmic chant of "I'm-going-to-the-circus! I'm-going-to-the-circus!" As I dressed for Mr. Bertram Mills's enterprise at Olympia my head rang to a similar refrain; only the words were different. "I'm-not-going-to-the-theatre! I'm-not-going-to-the-theatre!" was my burden. After the manner of that small youth who thought that he might like a copy of *The Pilgrim's Progress* for a birthday present, but knew, definitely, that he would prefer a squirt, I too often set out for the play knowing how much more surely I should enjoy the rough-and-tumble of the sawdust. Whereas the play is not always good, for me that other entertainment cannot be bad. And the less pretentious it is the better.

The circus at Olympia has every quality save the one which matters most—atmosphere. This is not Mr. Mills's fault; or at least it is a fault inherent in the magnitude of his conception. No man can hire the biggest hall in London, hold up the High Street with a criss-cross of Rolls-Royces and charge fifteen shillings for a stall, and yet hope to vie, in charm, with a page of *Les Frères Zemganno*, or the village show that springs up in the night. There enchantment takes on the true faery quality. It is a fascination compounded of trodden earth and smoky flares, of the sense of theatricality where no theatre should be, of intimacy with a race of people the farthest from the workaday. There wit is freely bandied between the wag of local reputation and the professed clown; there urchins lacking the wherewithal of legitimate entry make sneaking assault upon the canvas; there authority, in the shape of the circus attendant, displays a heavy and healthily soiled hand. Not all the perfumes of Coty can compete with the bruised odour of earth desecrated, yet glorified; a hundred arc-lamps cannot equal the radiance of that single wick of kerosene. Then what setting is the fashionable turmoil of Olympia compared with the bosom of the hills?

Since, however, it is an old mistake to complain of one thing that it is not another, I should do this handsome undertaking wrong were I to blame it for not having the merit of a paltry one. Let me say that it did for one moment attain to this peculiar merit. This was immediately after the performance, when we emerged from the inner temple into the profanity of the booths. A hoarse voice proclaimed that an artist, whom one had to suppose of lesser virtue than the elect of the ring, would now, free of charge, loop the loop on a bicycle. If you had a good place close to the barrier you could almost touch him, could with certainty appreciate the texture of his fleshings, note the ripple of his muscles, and revel in his immediate glamour. The apparatus of his performance was snail-shaped; and high up, where the horns are, was a little platform with a wooden bicycle. The acrobat climbed to the horns, mounted the machine, spat on his steady hands, and set off to gather breakneck speed in less than a trice. Interiorly he encircled the snail's house, a trap opened, and he was safe. This was for me the one thrill of the evening; for once the atmosphere was entirely right.

Given, however, that a circus at Olympia is by site and conditioning precluded from simplicity, I do not see that there was any other course except to pile up extravagance. A crescendo of effect being envisaged, we might, I think, have been first amazed by the smaller glories of tradition, and so become inured to the increasing marvellous. One missed the paper hoops, the bareback riders, the gallant fellows jumping at a venture. One looked in vain for the pair of cream-coloured steeds tearing round the ring bearing, each on its level quarters, a silk-shod petit-maître, the two forming a twin pedestal supporting a *Diane chasseresse*, all smirk and prink and coy retreat. There was none of this simple apprenticeship; instead, we were launched into the sheer incredible, and it was as though some tactless virtuoso were to begin his recital with that set-piece and recognised finale, Liszt's Rhapsodie Hongroise, No. 12. The Olympia circus aims to startle, and it ends by jading. Arithmetically I did not find it quite sound. The programme implied, for instance, that nothing could be funnier than the nine clowns. Yet one must think Grock funnier. Let it be admitted that each clown is one-ninth as funny as that supreme genius; their sum does not amount to Grock. Nor does the whole lunatic congress incline me to forget Auguste, forever helpful and forever in the way.

These reservations apart, the show was admirable. There was an exquisite Italian juggler. Everything that Rastelli did was simple in conception, yet infinitely difficult of execution. He juggled with none save beautiful things—fans, flowers, articles of virtu, skittles of fair shape and boxes of just proportion. Scornful of rehearsal, he arrived from Italy in time to jump into his silk and give a performance as flawless as Cinquevalli's and more decorative, so that with his physical beauty and youthful grace he gave the impression of an artist in whose mind there was a definite, almost concrete, conception of beauty. Eight Scotch collies whose training, the programme assured us, could only have been accomplished by kindness, performed a drama with every appearance of enjoyment; an English thoroughbred went through the paces of the *haute école* as though he had been foaled to that end; forty riderless horses moved in planetary decorum to the voice and whip of their master. (The restricted sugar supply of recent years has not, it would seem, affected our animal-trainers adversely.) Lockhart's Elephants, whose strength and long memory render any certificate as to gentleness of treatment unnecessary, appeared at their most Delsartian; Abdullah's Arab tumblers justified their swarthy race as no pale-faced Council with a mandate could ever hope to do. And then there were the aerial achievements of the Original Seigrist-Silbrons, "a company of absolutely fearless performers who defy the laws of gravitation". I am inclined to think that they do nothing of the sort, and that $V=gt$ is true for them as for us. That their cleverness consists in the skill with which, obedient to ascertained formula, they avoid catastrophe. To sum up, this circus, which was the most elaborate I have ever seen, was a fine example to theatrical producers of the inability of magnificence alone to create illusion. One would have given the whole of this great show for a little tent-pole in a little field! But Olympia is not a little field, and the show shone magnificently, according to its lights.

If I were asked which of all London's Palaces of Delight held for me the most of glamour, I should unhesitatingly reply: "The Agricultural Hall." From that day years ago when I, or rather the sweetest little filly that ever owned to three years, carried off two first prizes at the London Hackney Show, the Hall has been a paradise. But then, I have not squandered glamour; my secret has been to visit Islington strictly when enchantment has been scheduled, only I have spelt that word

H O R S E S. I have cold-shouldered the noblest professions, steered clear of draper and confectioner, miner and laundryman, paid heed neither to Mr. Grit the grocer, nor to Mr. Bung the brewer. In short, I have avoided the Hall whenever its main attractions have had fewer legs than four.

When that day came, then, when the editor of a great and noble paper besought me to take a pound note from his purse and spend it royally on the best entertainment in London—stipulating only that I should render, if not an accurate, at least a picturesque account—I had no hesitation. I hied me to the little underground dingle in Kingsway which I, personally, find so much more romantic than Sulby Glen. After expending 2d. or 3d.—in the excitement of the ride, I forgot to note which—and ninepence admission, I was up the slope and past a brand-new traction engine on a stand, looking proud as a rocking-horse in all his new-found glory of steel-grey and scarlet, with nineteen whole shillings to expend upon adventure, trumperies, and gauds.

First I yielded me to a palmist. "Scoffers particularly invited," said the Sibyl, shaking Titian-red locks covered with sequins. Bang went half a crown. "You are fond," said this soothsayer, who had at least the distinction of being the most fallible I had ever met, "you are fond of machinery!" This to me, who abominate motor cars, aeroplanes, and the whole ironmongerish caboodle! However, I reflected, people who draw bows at a venture must sometimes hit the wrong target, and I assured the prophetess that she was entirely right. "Don't you go being a naughty scoffer no more, then!" she rejoined, with an arch shake of the sequins.

Next I encountered a friendly camel posted as sentinel at the entrance to the menagerie. An interesting fellow, chewing his potato the exact number of times laid down by Mr. Gladstone for human mastication. But I left him and his four-footed brethren until I had disposed of the bipeds.

Now, when Horace said that the art of life was to *desipere in loco*, he probably meant that at a world's fair we must take things at their face value. That night, at Islington, I believed an incredible number of unbelievable things, beating to a frazzle Alice's White Queen, who, before breakfast, achieved no more than a meagre half-dozen. Before that night was over I managed a good hundred. I believed, for example, that the ethnologists are all wrong, and that the two magnificent

African negroes wearing headdresses of cocks' feathers were really Cherokee braves. I believed every word of the life-history which Togo, of the tribe of Moki Trogonyte Indians, sold me for a penny. I believed that rattlesnakes could bite him "impunely", that in his country the venom of poisonous snakes is administered to infants with their milk, that all the pennies contributed by us went, untouched by Togo, to the support of Togo's wife and fourteen children in the heart of Mexico. I believed in the fat woman and the dwarf, in all the magnificently variegated and exquisitely caparisoned humanity. I believed that, as I saw them in the show, so they lived outside; and refused only to credit that they must, at closing time, get them into shabby suits and indecent bowler hats, or accept that they, who from noon till close upon midnight had been as gods and eke goddesses, should now become plain men and women, even as you, reader, and I.

Next came the theatre, where, sitting upon an upturned gingerbeer box, I, like the mad king of Bavaria, was the sole spectator of a drama. A twentieth-century morality play, this! A young lady of blameless aspect was shown first in a pose reminiscent of Botticelli. "*Primavera della vita!* Oh, youth, oh, spring!" I cried. But the lady impresario who managed the curtain repressed my enthusiasm. Next little missy was shown examining an opium pipe. Next, in a pose of abandonment, holding aloft an empty bottle of Somebody's cider. "We are compelled to leave a good deal to the imagination!" said my mentor. "Of course," I murmured. "Health giving way, the Victim feels Remorse!" heralded a tableau which affected me deeply; but "Whilst there is Shame there is Hope!" seemed to me one of those things which might have been expressed differently. I am happy to say that the play came to an end in gloom deep enough to please even Mr. Drinkwater.

Let me not too boastfully recount how, with maximum intrepidity and skill at the darts, rings, quoits, and skittles, I became the possessor of a sugar basin, hot-water jug, and "binette"—I have sworn that once in my life I will use that vile word. Or too proudly relate how my steed ran a dead-heat for the Derby with that of the fellow at the next turntable—a "tough" of the most cut-throat description. Or how we ran it off, not only once but twice, the judge being still unable to separate us. "'Ere!" said the suspicious proprietor, "wot's all this? Are you two blokes in colloosion?" And giving us each a prize, he bade us be off. After a drink with the fellow of bloodthirsty mien who turned out to be a harmless baker's assistant, I returned to the menagerie. The catalogue gave no guarantee of accuracy, "as one or more of the specimens may die". Certainly "Prince", the forest-bred, black-maned African lion—heavenly description!—who lolled in one corner of his cage with his tongue despondently out, and was prodded to no protest by my stick, seemed mopish. Perhaps he was only bored. The cage opposite gave the lie to the poet's line about "tame and shabby tigers". "Dolly" was a resplendent creature, and seemed not tamed at all. I wish I had space to take you round all the cages. I would invite you to compare the coyote with your moneylender; the porcupine, who runs at his foe backwards, with your income-tax collector; the chattering monkey with the silent member for your constituency. You must imagine these and a hundred other delights. I shall not have room to say even half of what I would about the magnificent circus, complete with piebald horses and performing elephants, ringmaster, clowns, equestrians, and equestriennes, "dental gymnasts", trapeze artists who fell into the net from desperate heights, and so gave you the authentic thrill. For one hour I sat enthralled and recovered my youth. "Does earth hold a prouder destiny than that of the circus groom?" I was wont to ask my childish self. Even to-day I must think not.

I left the hall jingling three half-crowns, the handsome remainder of my editor's note. I left wondering many things. Whether Housman is not right about the littlest amount of mirth sufficing to restore man's soul: whether the sugar basin, hot-water jug, and slop basin, the trophies of my personal prowess, belonged to me or to the proprietor of my paper: whether I might rightfully expend those three half-crowns upon a supper commensurate with the glories of the evening. But most I wondered which could be the biggest bird in the world, since the menagerie catalogue had given the emu as the second largest, and the ostrich the third. I asked my tram conductor. But we were back again at the dingle, with no more helpful suggestion than the kangaroo.

(1923)

"True and Tender"

~~~~~~

"True and tender is the North land,
Fair and fickle is the South."

LANCASHIRE—a difficult county to love! One of the grimiest and grimmest. Yes, I realise that part of Windermere is in Lancashire, remember sunny hours spent at Clitheroe, and have not forgotten that I learned to weave under the lee of Pendle Hill. But Lancashire as a whole? Chimneys palling the countryside in the dunnest smoke of hell. A huddle of mean towns and chemical-ridden fields with white sheets bleaching on the chlorine-sodden hedge. And then the vision changes, and in the same fields daffodils begin to peer, and presently it is Saturday afternoon with League cricket and the sun shining. Even the pubs look less dingy now that the lawns at the back have their visitors. And what are all these old boys doing? Curiously inspecting their lasting home, as Stephen Phillips puts it? Not a bit of it. They are engaged in the game, art, mystery of bowls. And the gods on Olympus are not having a better time.

Now the year wears on to the season of horse shows and horse races, and to August. It is Bank Holiday, and all of Lancashire that has not gone to Leeds to do battle against Yorkshire has made assault upon Blackpool, where the tide rises less high than the spirits of your Lancastrian on holiday. But the hounds of winter are on autumn's traces, and soon Lancashire goes to the dogs resignedly and philosophically, but with the idea of picking a winner here and there. Now football rises like a fever in the blood, and the great day comes when Lancashire descends upon Wembley, and Londoners gaze upon strange hordes as though they were monkeys, not realising that it is they, the Londoners, who are behind bars. And perhaps that night at the Palladium our Gracie is singing. And then my county has another side —the intellectual and artistic side. The Hallé Concerts were giving Manchester undiluted Beethoven, Berlioz, Wagner, and Richard Strauss when London could not make up its mind whether the Eroica Symphony or a cornet solo was the proper thing to put between the Overture to *Zampa* and a selection from *The Gondoliers*. I do not insist on the Hallé Concerts as a rigidly Lancashire institution. They were kept going by the colony of German Jews headed by the great family of Behrens. But no German and no Jew had a finger in that august pie known as the *Manchester Guardian*.

"True and tender is the North land, Fair and fickle is the South," we used to sing on breaking-up day at the Manchester Grammar School. True, yes, but tender, no. Or perhaps I should say that the tenderness of my county is a long, long way beneath the surface. On leaving school I had for a year to catch the 8.33 train to Nelson to learn weaving at my father's mill. One morning I missed the train and took the 9.33, in front of which, shortly after it left Accrington, a man threw himself; at Rosegrove I saw the driver go round the engine with a taper to make sure that it had not been damaged! Students of coincidence may like to know that on one other occasion, and one only, did I miss the 8.33. Again I took the later train, and sniffing the morning air outside Bury saw a man rush from behind the bridge and put his head on the line. Relating this to my fellow travellers some weeks later I ended up with the banal reflection that no man can throw himself in front of the train in which he is travelling. "Tha'rt reet," said a man in the corner. "But tha can allus chuck thissen through bluddy winder!" One recollection leads to another. One day an extremely offensive Cockney started to bully a timid little commercial traveller. This, however, was quickly broken up by a stout man who appeared to be all stomach and watch chain. Speaking slowly he said to the bully: "Draw it mild, lad, or Ah'll punse thee. If tha weren't a Londoner, which means tha'rt daft, Ah'd punse thee from here to bluddy Christmas. And Ah'm not sure as Ah won't, next time bluddy train stops."

Yes, a passion for realism, unadulterated by any trace of sentimentality or even sentiment, is the clue to Lancashire character. "Hoo [she] looks gradely," said a condoler, viewing the body of his friend's dead wife. The husband retorted: "Ah should think hoo does look gradely. Hoo'd just had six weeks at Blackpool!" And here is a story which I have told in London many hundreds of times without once being understood. An old couple, the parents of a sickly child who is being given a week's holiday at the sea by a kind-hearted neighbour, are sitting silent after supper. Suddenly the wife says: "What's worriting thee, Bob?" And Bob says slowly: "Ah've thowt [thought], and Ah've thowt, and Ah've better thowt, and Ah conna see as how Mrs. Smith is going to be the better for taking our Alice to Morecambe."

But deep, deep down there is, I suppose, tenderness. One day during the dinner hour I was chatting with a lot of mill-hands outside the factory when we perceived a wretched spark of humanity wending its crippled way along the pavement like a toad with four club feet. As a signal that we should make way for this ruin, one of our number cried: "Hey up, a chap!" He recognised that here in God's sight was as much a man as the captain of the Cup-winning team we had been discussing.

"Aren't you a little out of your element, Mr. Hibbert?" asked a smarmy Levantine Jew meeting on the Manchester Exchange a yarn agent normally to be encountered on the Liverpool boards. Whereupon Hibbert, whose family helped to found both Exchanges, roared out of a lung capacity befitting his eighteen stone of good Lancashire brawn: "Out of my element, you bloody little Egyptian bastard! What about you? Why aren't you on the banks of the Nile, throwing bricks at crocodiles?" There is your true Lancastrian, who would throw bricks at Nineveh and Tyre if those antique cities put on airs with him.

One last story. In the 'seventies a poor wretch got caught up in the machinery of the great Samuel Rowbottom's mill. He was horribly mangled, and it took six yards of calico to hold the remains. "Thank you for the cloth, Mr. Rowbottom," said one of the stricken relatives, preparing to depart. "Thank you be b——d!" said old Rowbottom. "It'll be a shilling." But he sent a guinea wreath.

Here then are the reasons why I love my county. We invented the word "jannock", which means the square deal and no nonsense. We do not beat about the bush. We wrap up nothing. We do not care a tin hoot for anybody. We don't mind liking you, and we don't mind if you don't like us. We inhale tripe, and exhale fish and chips. We wear hard little hats on our hard little heads. We are as common as dirt. We are the salt of the earth, and you can do what you like with the sugar.

(1942)

Another Essay on the Comic Spirit

"A DIRTY mind," declared the Dook Snook in *Ally Sloper's Half-Holiday*, "is a perpetual feast." This is a motto, which, had I my way, would be emblazoned over the portals of every music hall in the kingdom. Only I should probably inscribe the word "healthy" and rely upon your Pantagruelist, who alone should be free of these temples, to catch at the Rabelaisian sense. The music hall is emphatically no place for the nice-minded, the makers of finical distinctions. It is essentially a place for the catholic. The great virtue of Rabelais is that he writes openly of those things which are commonly relegated to the privies of the mind. The great virtue of the music hall is that it jokes openly of those things which are commonly discussed in bar parlours. Whenever this openness is in any degree veiled we descend at once to that "durtie hypocrisie" which is the supreme offence.

These very obvious reflections are suggested by recent performances, at the Holborn Empire, of a music-hall artist to whom I am devoted, Miss May Henderson, and at the Victoria Palace of another artist to whom I am not devoted at all. Miss Henderson, the "Dusky Comedy Queen", makes no appeal to the dissembling mind. She provokes no furtive snigger. Her wit is not "near the knuckle"; it is the knuckle itself. The only possible excuse for her rib-ticklers is their outspokenness. Like Rabelais, her joking may be occasionally concerned with foul things, but it is never indecent. She "drags away the veil with a strong hand, does not leave impropriety half covered and so prompt the reader [spectator] to a filthy curiosity". In addition to its humour, the performance of this artist is of the highest technical excellence. Her songs go with the rattle of machine guns. There was one ecstatic moment when every person in the theatre proclaimed himself, with a huge shout, to be of the untrammelled company of Pantagruel. The only exceptions were those whose youth, as Stevenson quaintly says, had been depressed by exceptional aesthetic surroundings. Of such I glimpsed but two.

The quality of that other performance at the Victoria Palace was quite different. Superficially of a higher order of "gentility", it offended against Pantagruelism in that it provoked the imagination without intent to satisfy. The artist, who was enormously stout, made exhibition of a great deal of flesh. As a minor compensation she had the wit to provoke you to think she would have not resented comparison with Beardsley's drawing of the women in "The Wagnerites". Now there is no harm in bare flesh, but there was harm in her partner's jokes about nakedness—the harm of commonness. In its essence this was a performance for kitchen-maids. One does not resent kitchen-maids; they are useful people, and are entitled to entertainment. What one did resent was the *décor*, the expensiveness of such clothes as there were, the grand piano, the "drawing-room atmosphere". *Facetiæ* fittingly babbled over a slop-stone, or among bellying clothes-lines, were out of place. At the Holborn Empire, I had been less displeased by a child of, apparently, some seven summers, in baby-bonnet and baby-socks, delivering herself of such sophistications as:

> "There's a tavern in the town, in the town,
> And it's my town,
> It's not a dry town;
> I shall take my pals and my pa and ma
> To have a drop of whiskey in the old back bar,
> When I get back to my town, to my town."

This was nauseating, but at least the mind was untouched. Whereas what one felt about the grown-up performance was that it directly encouraged the grocer's assistant and the butcher's boy, if not to a more vicious way of living, at least to a commoner way of thinking.

In justice to the young gentleman in dress clothes who had helped to crack the jokes about nudity, let me record that when he was left to his own devices he sang, and sang very well, the good ballad, "Johnny Ludlow", and that the resultant applause was ten times greater than that evoked by his quips to lechery. The programme at the Holborn Empire included Mr. G. S. Melvin, who described himself as "The Versatile Comedian". Mr. Melvin did not strike me as being a comedian at all, but rather as an actor of exceedingly clever invention. It is no small feat to impersonate a figure of Bakst, a ship's stoker, and a blue-stocking at a University Extension lecture, all to the life and within half an hour. There was on the blue-stocking's startled countenance the ingratiating expression of the earnest female peering through pince-nez at improving truth. The stoker was remarkably true to life. Mr. Melvin is almost as graceful a dancer as Eugene Stratton, and it is a pity that he winds up some admirable acting with a poverty-stricken, sentimental song. There were also Mr. Fred Karno's comedians in *Mumming Birds,* at once a burlesque and the very stuff of the music hall. One of the comic gentlemen gave an "impression" of Sir Frank Benson as Mark Antony. "Sir Frank" forgot his words and substituted, not some happy froth blowing Shakespearianly about the surface of this actor's temperament, but a line from a well-known chorus of Miss Florrie Forde.

I have never seen anything quite so realistic as *The Rest Cure,* a play-let at the Holborn Empire. In five minutes I knew that here was a masterpiece. A sick man in pyjamas, carrying his boots and balancing a silk hat on the top of a red and tousled wig, suggests the comic as Mr. Karno's comedians understand it. And indeed, the invalid's antics are of that order. But they are built up on ideas, wee intellectual mice running about the foot of a mountain of grosser folly. There is the nurse who never comes into the room without insisting upon making up the bed. There is the solicitous friend whose newspaper opens at the story "Sad Death in a Nursing Home—Damp Sheets the Cause". We know, in dreams of farce wilder than the stage may give, that mourner who, taking the sleeper for dead, cannot decide how to dispose his flowers to advantage about the body, and that undertaker's man who, having taken his melancholy measure, finds his tape to be *wider* than the door. That these things should be so little funny on paper is good evidence of their theatrical effectiveness when you couple them with the fact that they sent the house into delirium. Each of the actors possessed an enormous sense of character. They were not just buffoons, but *buffo* incarnations of the sinister. In their funereal garb they stood out like puppets in a marionette show; and their actions took on all the super-consequence of puppets. Or you could liken them to those unfortunate attorneys, singing masters, pantaloons who, in Rossinian opera, are eternally fated to be thrust out of doors. There was thoughtful laughter here as well as pictorial burlesque. "Where did those flowers come from?" asked the aggrieved patient. "A bookmaker brought them!" replied the man of shrouds, preoccupied with his tape and that all-too-narrow door.

When I arrived at the Princes Theatre it was to find the house in delighted uproar over a comedy of manners performed by the brothers Griffiths, than whom Mr. Shaw declared the late James Welch could never be funnier. It was a question of a sleight-of-hand performance to which the more robust of the brothers, in the genteel get-up of a theatrical manager, was making conscientious objection. Perched upon that round bulletlike head, and significant of "the front of the house", was the authentic topper, a shade too small. But only a shade. The discrepancy, less than that connoted by caricaturists of Mr Churchill and Mr. George, was, indeed, of an extraordinary vrai semblance. The cylinder posed as coping-stone of the man of small successes, of one who has a snug sum put by. *Finis coronat opus.* The tile crowned a life work. Yet all was not well. The least spark of argumentative heat, and the hat would take a tilt over the nose to the extinction of rebuke. A gesture imperfectly restrained, and it would slither rearwards to discover a witless cranium. This dressy fellow and enforced equilibrist must walk delicately, with haviour protestant, static. Now adjustment is slight, now it gives place to magnoperative retrieval. Reiterant, the disputant picks up the thread of his discourse. He gets a sentence well under way and his countenance relaxes into security. He rounds his period and starts with confidence on the next. But his certainty is ill founded; he had done better to heed the famous advice of Heine to his countrymen: Above all, no emphasis! For now must he run the gamut of fearful apprehension—from the first shade of anxiety to the complete agony. Slowly the hat begins to decline over one ear. . . . O polish'd perturbation! silken care! Never once does the Mr. Griffiths, whom I take to be senior, descend to gross fooling; the quandary is from real life. So a civic worthy who has picked up the covering of a lesser brain. Coquelin's burgess was not more amusing, nor was the key of presentation greatly different. When, later, the brothers became a corporate horse of pantomime variety, they still kept in touch with the world of intellect. And here, surely, is the essence of supreme clowning, that it shall derive originally from the brain.

The next turn plunged us into the more dismal traditions of the British music hall. To wrest from the combined arts of music, costume, scene-painting, and the dance such utter joylessness as that prosecuted by the Palace Girls must have taxed the utmost genius of Mr. John Tiller. Doubtless these young people have talent and to spare; they but do as they are bidden. Nevertheless, I do not remember ever having seen dancers subjugated to such charmless behests. The interval was filled with an orchestral rehearsal of Sir Harry Lauder's familiar choruses. All around me was a tremor of anticipation. And then the curtain drew up to disclose, not Sir Harry, but an American-Indian

114

Princess, defined on the programme as a *prima donna*. This lady's native wood-notes wild were, one felt, inopportune. She should have sung herebefore. When, finally, her top F had trailed away, there was a gladsome rustle. The backcloth now drew up to show a vacant stage, and the house settled down for the little man.

Let it be said at once that there is nothing cringing about Lauder. He has the great artist's overweening conceit of himself. He emerges from the wings like the sun from base clouds. He irradiates this world, flattering stalls and gallery with sovereign eye. That a creature like ourselves should glow with such intensity of self-appreciation warms the cockles of the most sceptical heart. Here is one who tastes life to the full, and insists upon our tasting it too. He gives of his superfluity, willy-nilly, like a cup that runs over. His first item is all about a Clydeside gumph and his mistress, Bella the Belle of Dunoon. Lauder makes his lover hardly human. With his rude thatch, squat figure, dependent arms and warped legs, he recalls ancestral boughs. The actor insists wilfully upon this, executing between the verses a jocund step in parody of our father, the ape. It is not until the next song that you size up the artistry of the man. It is a different Lauder who, in the garb of an old salt, puts on the tenderest humanity. The verse is pure doggerel, the tune reminiscent of Mr. Chevalier's "My Old Dutch". Harmony is non-existent. Yet such is the intensity of the emotion conveyed that the whole house, simple and hypercritical alike, fall a-singing:

> "There is somebody wai-ai-ting for me
> In an old cabin down by the sea,
> In the land where I wish I could be
> There is somebody wai-ai-ting for me-e-e,
> There is somebody wai-ai-ting for me."

The composition is all Sir Harry's own, and I am to admit that it would seem to be the singer's proper, unsimulated emotion which produces the spontaneous and magical effect. And yet the man's an actor. Shade of Diderot and his accursed paradox!

Lamb was wrong when he said that the school of Munden began, *and must end*, with himself. Lauder is in the direct line of Munden. Can any man "wonder" like Lauder? Can any man "see ghosts" like him, or "fight with his own shadow" as he does? "She'll be full of surprises, In the morning when she rises, To hear I'm in the town," he sings, and as at the word "surprises" he drops his voice to a whisper, Lauder conjures up a poet's vision of first rapture. So Lucy thinking on Richard Feverel. "She laid on my waistcoat, close to my heart," contains the core of "Hang there like fruit, my soul, Till the tree die!" There is a deeper wonder here, surely, than the older actor possessed, or so we must believe. But Mundenish in its quiddity is the picture of Doughie the baker, ruminating on the jealousy of his spouse. Doughie describes the two houses and the narrow passage between them as graphically as you would want to describe them to a child. He makes you see the two abodes as they were the painted arks of twin Noahs. The baker was coming home to his tea just as his neighbour, Mrs. McCulloch, emerged upon an errand. They met in the passage "like two trams". "Mind ye", says Doughie with superb, irrelevant insistence, "I canna tell ye what Mrs. McCulloch was going oot for!" The whole of this patter is crowded with particularities which give it credibility. Old favourites followed, and then Sir Harry showed us that doubling of the artist which, on the stage, is least pleasing. He gave an unaccompanied, maudlin song, and a little homily on the blessings of peace.

It must not be supposed that Lauder does not calculate his effects. He does. Each verse is more elaborate than the preceding one, so that the result is both cumulative and culminative. The actor has an exceedingly fine feeling for character. Soldier, sailor, yokel, God's innocent are all to their several manners born. They are true to nature, yet transfigured. Even Doughie, the loutish baker, his face covered with flour, his brow bound with a ragged bonnet, wears about him something elfin, something of Pierrot. Once or twice the daft fellow will cock a malignant eye, and in such a moment the great actor is revealed. Lauder can make a face of horror like the mask of Irving's Dante confronted with the starving Ugolino. These qualities of pathos and tragedy, like the wistfulness of Chaplin, are not what the generality look for. To them Lauder is a figure of pure fun with a modicum of sentimental alloy. They love that description of Bonnie Wee Jean with her velvet arms round her father's neck, but they adore still more that rueful "But she's got ma nose and ear-r-r-s!" Here again the comic idea is given an ingenious twist. The gist of it is not the superimposing of absurdity upon plain sense, but the discovery of the rational in lunatic or sentimental disguise. When all is said and done the man remains an evangelist whose tidings are of pure Celtic joy.

Continually one hears expressions of regret at the passing of the music hall. The Palladium has gone over to revue, the Palace to "the pictures"; either betrayal, apparently, contents the Empire. Even the Euston has fallen, and into aestheticism's very maw. This gives me for Mr. Nigel Playfair that tempered animosity which one feels for the friend who would protect you, willy-nilly, against your lower self, who would bar the way to a pleasant, familiar vice. An enterprise so single in pursuit of pleasure as the music hall, so avowedly free from moral implications, cannot, the Puritans tell us, be contained within a more polite category. These good people fail to realise that vice and virtue have one thing in common: repress them in one place and they break out in another. Were I to attempt a parallel between this continual chivvying of the music hall and the harassing of the early Churches, I should want to make one point very clear. This point is that persecution, although admittedly the most favourable of soils, is still not more than the mould round the roots of the plant which, if it is to flourish, must contain within itself the vital seeds. Sects and denominations have prospered in the face of persecution simply because there was a genuine demand for their creeds. The music-hall managers have sought to do away with the music-hall programme in the belief that there is no further demand for it. They are wrong. People still want that programme, and will, I submit, continue to want it whenever it is as good as that presented at the Victoria Palace.

All juggling is beautiful, though different performers belong to different orders in beauty. Rastelli, making of that immemorial trinity of the juggler, his cigar, gloves, and umbrella, a Catherine wheel of beauty, brings to the mind something of the sculptor's sense of rhythm. Mr. Bert Elliott, with his "Topsy-Turvy Toppers", does not soar so high, content with bringing off the feat announced and careless of the finer shades. He throws his three top hats into the air, catching each one on his head in turn so that it executes between forehead and cranium a little dance like that of a spun coin returning to a state of rest. There is a future here for these discarded insignia; our old bonnets are put to their right use, the juggler's head. Rastelli would have made of this trick a glossy symbol of the eighteen-nineties; Mr. Elliott declines upon the beauty of efficiency. His technical mastery is, we may think, of the same order as Mr. Mark Hambourg's; none could have played these variations on a theme of top hats more accurately or with a more surpassing swiftness.

The next turn takes us into high life. It is called "Symphonia: A Combination of Instrumental and Vocal Harmony". The curtain rises to disclose a magnificent interior modelled on the Socialist conception of the home life of the idle rich. Disposed about a saloon of which the spaciousness is accentuated by a grand piano and some standard palms, an obvious baronet and his three daughters take their after-dinner ease. They are in evening dress. The eldest daughter presides at the piano, the next in staidness nurses her 'cello, the youngest and most frolicsome cuddles a violin. These young ladies care little, apparently, for music in which they can all join, say the simpler Beethoven trios, preferring to entertain Papa with soli of incredible virtuosity. She who plays the violin leads off with a piece of dull persistence, a "Perpetuum Mobile", which I cannot assign to any known composer. This itch for discovery must run in the blood, since presently the 'cellist takes up the search with something I assign to Popper. And now that other Poppa, the head of the household, intervenes. The widower—for such, alas! I take the Baronet to be—clears his throat, the lights are lowered, and he plunges into the thick of his ballad. It is not an old song and it is not a new one; it impales us on the horns of the old Spencerian dilemma of the created or the self-created universe. We cannot imagine the time when either the music or the words were not. It is, perhaps, a lawful conception that in the beginning both were and rushed together, sentimental oxygen and hydrogen, to form the water of our tears. I may reproduce here only the words, the music you must deduce; it is inevitable, and follows the law of mass emotion:

"There's the road that is rough and stony,
        And it's uphill night and day;
    No stile to rest a little while,
        It's a tough road all the way.
    There's the road that is all sunshiny,
        It's the road we love to roam,
    But the road that leads [*pause*] to Heaven all
                the while
        Is the road to Home, Sweet Home."

This is received with the most rapturous acclaim, and really I like it quite as well as Mascagni's Intermezzo, the opening phrase of which is softly warbled behind the drawing-room's *portière*. And then a fourth and favourite daughter appears. The Baronet strikes the attitude which Orchardson has laid down for the widower's guidance, and we know that we are listening to her mother's voice. A hush falls upon the house, and I shall not quarrel with you if you say that this Italian treacle, too cloying for any palate of refinement, is yet healthier than the stupefying liquor distilled by the American negro from the gum of his native Jazz tree. The velvet curtains fall and the Baronet's musical evening is at an end.

Mr. Nelson Keys, who follows, is an interloper from a world of which the perceptions are alleged to be finer. This actor possesses the gift which has been lost to us since little Robson; he has the secret of that art of travesty which heightens the emotion of the thing travestied. His portrait of senility succumbing to Jazz is both ludicrous and terrible; this figure of old age dancing to the grave might have come straight out of an old-fashioned morality. I am tempted to say that this little inch is worth the entire canvases of some more consequential actors. Mr. Keys lets you see the world on a thumb-nail. The sublime of intellectual fooling is reached with his Cook's guide, rapturously seized at the moment of shepherding a party through Trafalgar Square, "a favourite resort of those so wittily described as the working classes". Tears of mirth stream down our faces as we watch the vagaries of that ragged moustache, and listen to that voice now booming like Big Ben when a strong wind blows up the river, now echoing the hollow wash of the tide receding from Fingal's Cave. An extravagant image? Mr. Keys is an extravagantly funny actor. On an entirely different plane is Mr. George Bass, who describes himself as "The Popular Comedian". "Popular" is entirely just; the people love him. "I like your socks, George," says the conductor. "Them's not socks," George replies, pulling up his trousers to show ankles encased in circlets of scarlet wool. "Them's mittens!" The quality of the fun here is what the French call *tordant*; the audience literally twists itself for joy. Mr. Bass is of Formby's school, the apparent simpleton who is "all there". With solemnity he declaims:

> "For East is East and West is West,
> Though the fact seems hardly relevant . . ."

The audience holds breath at the last portentous word, and needs it all for the immense guffaw released by the concluding

"Yet anybody knows you can milk a cow,
But you can't mess about with an elephant."

Let me add that the programme also contains Miss Ella Shields, straight as a ramrod in her policeman's and naval officer's uniforms, some trick cyclists and other tumblers. How, then, with all this actual joy and entire absence of tedium, should people not want the music hall? I want it, and shall go on wanting it—Baronet and all.

(1923)

No Worlds to Conquer

A GREAT evening at the Albert Hall. This was the fight for the bantam-weight championship of England, in which Teddy Baldock of Poplar beat Archie Bell of America and so brought back a title to the Old Country after thirteen years. It was the first time my companion had been in the Albert Hall, and he wondered what the Prince Consort and Queen Victoria and Felix Mendelssohn-Bartholdy and Sir Theodore Martin would have made of the assembly. The crowd were indeed an extraordinary lot, which an interval between the fights gave us leisure to observe. A charming little man with a cranium as stiffly denuded as an old campaigner's hairbrush, a cauliflower ear, and dainty manners, was engaged in conversation with a prince of the blood. Next to the prince was a famous writer of stories, with a pleated silk shirt, a curl, and in his twinkling eyes an implication that the boxers did not really know their business. Next to the novelist was the sallow and spirited author of the season's most successful play. Next to him a bunch of heads belonging to a surgeon, a cartoonist, a tailor. Next to this trio an equerry. Behind the equerry a pianist. With the pianist were a painter, a duke, a retired general, an active brewer, a judge of the High Court, a pushing shopkeeper, a sporting journalist, and a simple man-about-town. This completed the dapper little man's dapper little party.

I have little patience with those who cannot find dramatic excitement in the boxing ring. The clash of indomitable wills, the striving of spirit with spirit, the husbanding of energy until the time when the expense and drain of every faculty of mind and body are the only true economy—is not all this as much a part of drama as the story of the Theban king who slays his father and weds his mother? The tale of Œdipus is but a restatement of the primitive myth: the young year, which is the son, slays the old year, which is his father. Why, pray, should not a prize fight mirror the vicissitudes of the annual life of nature? Is it not also the old showing of one down, t'other come up? Curiously enough, the modern prize ring, with its raised platform surrounded by spectators, is the nearest thing that we have to the Elizabethan stage. The boxers disport themselves and play their parts among the company. Watching them, we behold a tragedy—for there is something tragic about the fall of a champion, be it only at skittles or shove-halfpenny—which is not only being acted for the first time, but is in no way blunted by rehearsal. You can be sure that the actors are in earnest, that they will not, as some other players do, run through their parts. Nor does any man know the upshot of this drama, whereas the catastrophe of *Hamlet* was known beforehand to the author, to Burbage, his company, the stage hands, and a lot of tedious underlings. Whether any play is a good play must always be a matter of private opinion, whereas a good fight is a matter of public fact.

Like Thomas Hickman, Mr. Archie Bell learned the first of all lessons—that Man was made to mourn. Hickman "lost nothing by the late fight but his presumption; and that every man may do as well without! By an over-display of this quality, however, the public had been prejudiced against him, and the knowing ones were taken in." There was much talk at the Albert Hall of an interview in which Bell had foretold the overthrow of the English pretender; which interview did, I think, at the beginning, prejudice the public against him. But this prejudice was soon overcome and borne down by the fighting gallantry of the American, who gave one of the best-tempered displays ever seen in this sporting country. "Every inch a little gentleman!" said a voice as Baldock, fine, drawn, thin, tall for his nineteen years, with a shock of auburn hair and a pleasant, modest bearing, climbed the steps, ducked beneath the ropes, and took his corner. Bell, a sturdy, well-built fighting man, of full growth and well muscled up, had not been fighting five minutes before the same voice said: "Two gentlemen in the ring! It's going to be a clean fight!" And a clean fight it was.

Frankly, if the American had beaten Baldock it would have been well-nigh unbearable. Youth will be served, and the young generation persists in knocking at the door. But need that youth be quite so young as Baldock? And though at the end of those thin arms there was a punch like the kick of a mule, might not Bell prove too stout a door for this battering? I go back to my original thesis and maintain that the frenzy for Baldock was as much emotional as patriotic. Alexander, though he had taken part in one or two "eliminating contests", was turned twenty before he stood with his army on the Plains of Thessaly. At twenty Frederick the Great trembled before his father and suffered exile in disgrace. Napoleon at twenty was a struggling author, writing Letters on the History of Corsica, and with no thought of escape into a larger world. Let not these comparisons be smiled at. No man can conquer a bigger world than that which is open to him; and what continents and the entire globe were to those others this championship was to Baldock. Success in the prime of life is admirable; yet success is what the prime of life is for. But to seize the glittering crown when you are still young enough to prize crowns and glitter and know nothing of their emptiness—this is the domain of pure romance. And this was the reason why, when the gong put an end to the age-long suspense of those last two rounds, every man in the hall, young and old, felt that though the voice was the voice of the referee, the goddess responsible for the reward was the Muse of Poetry. Crowded tier after crowded tier rose at the victor, who left the ring as modestly as he had entered it.

The spectators rose at Baldock because he had given proof not only of extraordinary skill—to which quite ordinary men can attain —but of that valour which is beyond the reach of any save the valiant. As experts reckoned the fight, the Englishman had established a handsome lead at the end of the fifth round. In the eighth it seemed that he had the American all in, and that Bell was saved by the gong. In the tenth round both men decided to indulge in a mix-up, and in this round honours were even. The eleventh, twelfth, and thirteenth rounds still saw Baldock tap, tap, tapping with his left; but his blows had lost some of their weight, while Bell was getting his counters home. Nevertheless, it was agreed on all sides that Baldock had a more than winning lead, and that, if he could keep his feet to the end, the match must be his. Then came the two last unforgettable rounds. In the fourteenth the American drove a magnificent right to Baldock's heart which shook the Englishman so much that for the rest of that round he fought purely by instinct and without any clear sense of what he was doing. Yet, even in this condition, he sent over a beautiful right, which nearly finished the match. In the fifteenth and last round Baldock took unnecessary chances. His opponent was obviously seeking the knock-out which alone could serve him, and, if the truth must be told, Baldock gave him every opportunity of finding it. Instead of being content to stall off his desperate, and by now stronger opponent, the coming champion gave his adversary the fight he wanted, but was on his feet when at last the gong struck. Perhaps, after all, the best form of defence is attack. But there were thousands in the hall who held their breath as the boy went after the boxer's equivalent for "a peerage or Westminster Abbey". Hazlitt appends a postcript to his account of the fray between the Gas-man and Bill Neate: "Toms called upon me the next day to ask me if I did not think the fight was a complete thing? I said I thought it was." I suggest that the fight in the Albert Hall was a complete thing. For one night this young Englishman was a-tiptoe on the highest point of being. He was nineteen and Champion of England. Though he should decline to the humdrum corner of some blowzy pub, nothing can take this from him that at nineteen he composed his *Meistersinger* and wrote his *Lear*.

Of all the prize-fights of recent times, the one that has excited me most was that between the Bombardier and Joe Beckett. Other fights I remember vividly enough though not with the same passion. There was Welsh's cold, scientific defeat of Ritchie, and Carpentier's lucky win over Gunboat Smith. Both events took place at Olympia shortly before the war, and drew their quota of fashionable ladies and elegant trollops, gold-toothed niggers, fops, clergymen, shop-assistants, artists. At this "venue"—as the newspapers call it when the prices are high enough—was the "clash" between Jimmy Wilde and Pal Moore, the fighting a foregone conclusion to that Celtic soul who brought from his native coal-fields an enormous dragon-embroidered flag with which to cover victor and vanquished in one hurly-burly of confusion and glory. Jimmy is no longer the wistful figure of frailty he once was. I have an early photograph in which he wears his yonderly expression, that air of not being strong; his features at that time had well adorned the fly-leaf of a story by George Macdonald. There was the remote, faint atmosphere of the Sunday school about him; he was a Donal Grant, an Alec Forbes. To judge by the colour of his hands, the little fellow might have posed after a day's work in the mine. Or say that he had been put up in his buff to fight a bully—the sport of some Saturday afternoon. Forked radish is too much a symbol of mass to denote his physique of those days. To-day Mr. Wilde takes his oysters and champagne like a man. He fills his clothes and so shrinks to life-size. He has ceased to be the wonder and the marvel of the age. He ranks with the world's workaday talents, and has become a journalist like myself. He has become reckonable; he does the things grown men may do, and not those which it were unthinkable a child should attempt. Other great events of the ring have I seen—Jim Driscoll's "tragedy"; Basham's woeful attempt to stand up against "Kid" Lewis; that hero's nine-seconds' dismissal of "Frankie" Moody; the unreflective pitting of rival beeves which was the fight between Goddard and Moran; Beckett's long-drawn agonies with M'Goorty and Mc-Cormick; encounters Blackfriars-way, where, in the ring, the blood is up indeed and, on the surrounding benches, admiration struggles with cupidity in the sharp-set, cunning faces of the "butchers from Tothill Fields, brokers from Whitechapel."

Yet not one of these matches had the same quality of apprehension as the Wells-Beckett affair. The result was never in doubt and yet seemed dreadfully to matter, though I agree that the issue of, say, the affray at Jutland was fraught with graver consequences than this battle of bruisers. May the Bombardier forgive me; but he is that, in spite of his auburn, close-curled hair, his courtesy and charm. Phoebus Apollo turned Promethean pug! Wells gives you the impression that his heart has long ceased to beat. He is fey, he cannot win; he will stave off defeat, gallantly, for an all too small number of rounds. He is "an absolute gentleman, full of the most excellent differences, of very soft society and great showing." And that is why he is foredoomed. Wells has everything that a gentleman should have, and nothing that a prize-fighter must own. In his book Carpentier wrote: "Wells is without what I call personality, a fighting personality." (He goes on to explain that to worry and jolly an opponent, to get on his mind as an obsession in the days of preparation before a match, is part of the "psychology" of the game. But then Georges had been staying in America.) Wells makes pretence to defy augury. Yet he knows that if defeat be not now, it will come; what is it then to lose betimes? Not much to him, perhaps, but to his friends an abiding sorrow. About Beckett there is no air of mystery. He glowers in his corner, and peering through little screwed-up eyes, appears to glimpse a big thing in front of him, to bend up every corporal agent to pull it off. For the rest he is a plain, blunt man, slow to give or take offence.

One of the most deeply rooted things in the English character is the love of sailors and prize-fighters. "Almost everybody in our land, except humanitarians and a few persons whose youth has been depressed by exceptional æsthetic surroundings, can understand and sympathise with an admiral or a prize-fighter. I do not wish to bracket Benbow and Tom Cribb; but, depend upon it, they are practically bracketed for admiration in the minds of many frequenters of alehouses. If you told them about Germanicus and the eagles, or Regulus going back to Carthage, they would very likely fall asleep, but tell them about Harry Pearce and Jem Belcher, or about Nelson and the Nile, and they put down their pipes to listen." Thus Stevenson.

And so it came about that on the night of combat all roads led to Olympia. The previous day had been Sunday, and Sunday's peace had been routed by the din of the impending conflict. You could not pick up a news-sheet without having it forced upon you that Mr. Wells was "quietly confident", and that Mr. Beckett was in the habit of saying nothing but grimly shooting out his lips. The men themselves do not advertise. But the newspapers have their self-respect, bless you, and see to it that heroes lose nothing by a Quakerish reserve. They make wonderful play with the "human interest", do our papers, with Mr. Beckett's stolidity and Mr. Wells's nerves. Arrangements were made to flash the news of the result all over England,

> "Till Belvoir's lordly terraces the sign to Lincoln sent,
> And Lincoln sped the message on o'er the wide Vale of Trent,
> Till Skiddaw saw the fire that burned on Gaunt's embattled pile,
> And the red glare on Skiddaw roused the burghers of . . . Southampton."

On Solent's shore that night there was no question of bed until the screen erected in the street had spoken. On that momentous night no lad throughout the length and breadth of the land went ignorant to his blankets; in the London clubs, at two in the morning, peers of the realm fought the battle over again. Next day all old bucks whose hearts were still sound turned first in their papers to the news that mattered. All hearts were with Wells. "I have taken the depth of the water," said Admiral Duncan, "and when the *Venerable* goes down my flag will still fly." The Bombardier knew that he must go down; but he had taken the depth of public esteem and knew that his flag would still be flying.

Wells is no coward; he was not nervous in the sense that he feared defeat. It was the thought of victory which unmanned him. He was like that cricketer fainting on the verge of a century, who faced the first ball without a tremor. History does not lack instances; so Hackenschmidt when he beat Madrali. A journalist of the period tells us that as the wrestlers were due to leave their dressing-rooms the news went round that the great Russian had an attack of nerves. His stomach was wrong! They were anointing him with alcohol! He was faint! He was trembling! And yet you would have sworn the huge fellow's nerves to be those of an ox. "It may be that coarse metals are less

126

flexible than finer; certain it is that they do not well cohere." It may be that this is true in mineralogy—philologists will know whether I mean metallurgy—it is not true in MAN. Wells was the finer metal of the two, finer in the sense of being the more sensitive, but it was Beckett who cohered and Wells who, in sporting parlance, came unstuck. But then he had gone to pieces before the fight began. It is said that the champion, shooting out his lips, pushed aside one of his seconds who was framing to ascend the steps before him. I did not notice this. What I did observe was a self-hypnotised Wells rooted to earth at the ring-side, his seconds patting the ladder to encourage him to mount. He was morally defenceless; it was as though his opponent held a sword in his hand against an unarmed body. And yet he did pretty well; he returned blow for blow, stalled off ruin, raised hopes, was battered to his knees. . . .

What is the secret of the hold Wells has always had over the British? Why have we leaned so tenderly to this reed shaken by the wind of every fighter's fist? Why, when the boards "received his hams and body", as a Georgian poet has it, have they received one who must always be a national hero? Perhaps it is because his is the head upon which "all the ends of the world are come". Perhaps, mischievously, because the beauty of Wells is a beauty wrought out from within upon the flesh, the deposit, little cell by cell, of strange thoughts and fantastic reveries. Set it for a moment before one of those tall goddesses and beautiful heroines of antiquity, and how would they be troubled by this beauty, into which the soul with all its maladies has passed. Like the vampire he has been outed many times, and learned the secrets of the grave; and trafficked for strange belts with fighting Frenchmen; and all this has been to him but as the sound of lyres and flutes. . . .

They wrapped Wells up in that dolorous dressing-gown which he was wont to doff so despairingly whenever the lights went up, and don so cheerfully as soon as his light was out. "It hurts," said his chief supporter after the fight. "It hurts, but there can't be two winners." This is the philosophy proper to such occasions. So Peter Jackson, negro and gentleman, after he had knocked out Slavin.

Jackson: "Good-night, Paddy. There can't be two winners, but good luck to you."

Slavin: "Good-night, Peter."

*　　*　　*　　*

It is the smaller fry to whom my heart most leans. It is meat and drink to me to see a second-rater. One gets tired of the big men, of their preening and peacocking, of their portentousness. I mislike the air of coming down to the arena horsed by captive kings. There is too much solemnity at Olympia, and the crowd is too well-behaved. In the smaller booths the little chaps dive in and out of the ring like fishes, without ceremony at the start, without too great a degree of elation or discomfiture at the finish. It would seem sometimes as though getting down to weight were with them not a part of training but an economic shift. They can be desperately thin. They are of all trades, blacksmiths, porters, fishmongers, newsboys, but common to them all are the badges of the heroic profession—the matted hair plastered low on the narrow forehead, the ringed and shaven neck, the felicitous devices of the tattooist. Stunted though they may be in intelligence, these budding bruisers can never be as inept as the polite young gentlemen who posture in revue. I cannot imagine a more honourable career than to knock-out and be knocked-out; I cannot conceive a less noble one than to loll life away on plush divans in company with eleven other scented and manicured little masters. I am conscious of some unfairness here. What alternative is there for the beauty-chorister? Selling gloves over a counter, making up posies at the florist's, barbering—all these demand a higher education, clerking calls for greater intelligence, and portering for greater physical strength. We should, perhaps, be prepared to forgive these little mannikins that they jig, amble and lisp; they might starve else. But their principals! Consider the highly-paid hero of musical comedy who sings a ditty in lawn-tennis flannels and yachting cap, and another or even the same ditty in dress-clothes and an opera-hat. Strip him of flannels and dress-clothes and, bless me, how little remarkable he would look! Strip your boxer, and he rises to the pristine dignity of man; clothe him, and he falls from his high estate. The queasy cap, the muffler, the coat with three buttons crowded together in the pit of the stomach, the tight trousers, the boots of soft uppers and snubbed toecaps—what uniform of degradation is this!

Boxers are they who, clothed, are in their wrong mind. Strippen out of rude array, they are men who realise that complete ferocity may go hand in hand with perfect amity. I remember being present at a small provincial show at which a lad was disqualified for biting. There was the usual uproar; the livery of shame was declared thenceforth the offender's only wear; there was talk of taking away his living. After the fight I took occasion to touch delicately, gingerly even, upon the subject of his trespass. The lad assured me with many fervent protestations that he had been totally unconscious of the action. He, if I may so express it, "sw'elp-me'd" into conviction of his moral innocence. "Besides", said he, "lor' lumme, I were winnin' any'ow! Got 'im set, I 'ad. Easy! There'd 'av bin no sense in bitin', an' that. I must 'a wanted to knock the grin off 'is ugly dial, see? Sw'elp me, that's stright! That's 'ow I looks at it, see? Wivout finkin'." And, surely, wilful biting under extreme excitement is more the act of a sportsman than the cold-blooded rigging of a fight. Perhaps these small shows are least admirable in their best-paid bouts. I once saw a French boxer, proffering a helping hand to one of our own brutes half-toppled through and tangled-up in the ropes, rewarded with a vicious blow in the mouth. The Frenchman was equal to the occasion. "Si c'est comme ça!" he said with a shrug, and resigned the fight. The referee at these contests needs to be a man of courage; a ginger-beer bottle hurled from the gallery is a formidable missile. A man of courage he is, therefore. When he sees a dazed and beaten man hang helpless on the ropes, and knows that in the din no voice can make itself heard, when, in this extremity, he bids Time advance a full minute and strike upon the bell, it is with the thronged circle of spectators as though another Joshua had ordered the sun to heel.

(1936)

A la Recherche

SOME little time ago I was strolling down one of those mean streets with which the British are careful to surround their more important buildings. It is almost as though "the authorities"—whoever they may be—begrudged the nation its Museum. Of all places in London this Temple of Knowledge is, to the provincial and the foreigner, the least accessible. Tramcars eschew it, buses pass it by. That is to say, they do not pass by it. Alight at the Tube station miscalled Museum, ascend to the upper air, and there is still no sign of any Temple.

There is an old and untrue story about an Englishman who inquired of a Strasbourger the way to his cathedral. "You take," said the docile Teuton, "the first to the right and the second to the left. This will bring you to a square at one corner of which is a tobacconist's. The cathedral is in the middle." The Londoner might say the same. He would tell you to get out at the station called Museum, to take the first to left or right—I can never remember which—execute a rear movement, turn round several corners till you come to a curiosity shop. "Opposite," he would say, "is what you are looking for."

I was gazing abstractedly into the windows of this aforesaid curiosity shop, and pondering upon the extraordinary workings of the British mind, when my eye fell upon the most entrancing vision of loveliness I have ever beheld. The object was an ordinary photograph taken by the ordinary, i.e. fashionable, photographer, whose sitters seem to be confined entirely to the highest circles of the nobility and stage. There was a time when the illustrated magazines were not quite so lavish in their presentment of the social and theatrical world as they are to-day. The public starved for want of images of those whom it held dear, and there was an enormous demand for cabinet photographs, at, I think, two shillings each.

I continue to gaze in that shop window. The vision which now enthralls me, and holds me literally spellbound, is Ellen Terry as she first appeared to my boyish gaze. She is wearing a simple white frock, and looking down over a plaster-of-Paris balcony. I cannot be sure about the piece; perhaps it is *The Amber Heart*. But what does it matter? Antique time holds no rapture like that which was Ellen Terry in the days of my youth. A great Spanish singer who had travelled the world over once told me that eighty years had not shown him any loveliness comparable to that April morning—sunshine and tears—which was Ellen.

Ellen Terry's features were, perhaps, not beautiful in the classical sense—that is, measured with a tape. But they spoke of better things than regularity; of gladness, heart, and wit. Not long ago the great actress supped at the house of an old friend of mine, who, with infinite care, prepared to put his honoured guest, all muffled up against the cold, into her cab.

"Boost me in!" she said in that voice like plum-coloured velvet. The driver spoke.

"H'and the lidy as I've the h'onour ter drive is Miss h'Ellen Terry! Larst time I see'd yer, mum, was at the Lyceum, in 1887. In the *Amber 'Eart* if yer remember!"

"There now, Courtenay," she said, "I told you I hadn't altered!"

"Got any old photographs, stage beauties and that sort of thing?" I asked the shopkeeper carelessly, with my heart in my mouth. I felt that, at cost of no matter what regret, I must not go beyond ten guineas.

"We've got Sir Johnston Forbes-Robertson when he was plain Mister."

"Let's have a look at him."

And Mr. Forbes-Robertson stands forth, in doublet and hose, and the air which he wore for Gratiano, Mercutio, or some graceful Veronese. He is mine for two shillings.

"There's Vesta Tilley about the same date."

And a portrait is produced showing that darling in 1902—was it? She is singing "Welcome, C.I.V.s", wears a waistcoat quartered with our country's arms, and carries the Union Jack aloft at the end of a dandy's cane. I go to half a crown for Vesta.

"Isn't that Ellen Terry in the window?" I breathe tremblingly.

"She's more," is the reply. "I can't let *her* go under five bob."

"Lyceum, 1887," was written on the back.

Yesterday I was entertaining a few people to lunch in my most modest of flats. The talk turned upon *Our Betters*, and the shimmering beauty and talent of Miss Margaret Bannerman. With her was contrasted Miss Constance Collier, whose splendid sullens and mutinous air were declared by one of her sex up to putting Herod in his place. The talk veered to Miss Gladys Cooper, Miss Isobel Elsom, Miss

Barbara Hoffe, June, and might have constituted a "legend of fair women".

I rose, went to the mantelpiece, took down the photograph, and placed it on the table.

There was a moment's silence. Then one spoke.

"That's different!" he said.

And I think that when the poet wrote of "the glory and the dream" he meant no more.

"Different"—that's all.

At the same time that I became possessor of the photograph of Ellen Terry I bought an old scrapbook, a huge affair of some two hundred pages. A single glance revealed that it was full of dramatic criticisms of a bygone day. When I got the book home I discovered that it had been consecrated to Henry Irving and Ellen Terry, and contained all the important notices of the productions at the Lyceum for a period of ten years. Also all the great actor's speeches and discourses. I judge from the extreme care with which the book is put together, the skill in dovetailing, arranging and pasting, the neatness of the dating and the omission to give the names of the papers, print to a woman being just print—I judge from all these that the compiler was a maiden lady, on the shadier side of forty. The articles so carefully culled cover a period from 1881 to 1890—the hey-day of the Lyceum Theatre. They are from all the more serious London journals of the period, plentifully relieved by the comic Press. The first play noticed is *The Belle's Stratagem*; the last, Mr. Henry Arthur Jones's *Judah*.

On an early page we find *Punch* apologising for the shortness of its notice, and regretting that it can find room for no more than the great actor's "too utterly precious legs", as the impressionable young ladies of the period called them. This is followed by an account of the banquet offered to the owner of the legs at the St. James's Hall on 4th July 1883. The occasion was the actor's forthcoming American tour. The Lord Chief Justice (Lord Coleridge) presided, and had the American Minister (the Hon. J. Russell Lowell) on his other side. At the top table were the Rt. Hon. Joseph Chamberlain, M.P., Professor Tyndall, Mr. J. L. Toole, and Mr. Alma Tadema, R.A. The menu consisted of turtle soup à la Prince de Denmark, salmon with Othello sauce, fillets of sole à la Jingle, chicken à la Macbeth—"All my pretty chickens and their dam at one fell swoop," says Macduff—quails cooked according to Richelieu's liking, ducks as Robert Macaire would have them, a salad after Benedick's heart, and a mayonnaise to please that rascal Dubosc. Ladies were privileged to look on from above while their lords feasted; a picture shows Miss Terry reclining under a palm. As befitting these more delicate vessels, refreshments in the balcony consisted of ices and strawberries and cream. The compiler of my scrapbook religiously kept and pasted in the counterfoil of her ticket, showing that she occupied seat No. 91 in row No. 2 in the balcony. Next to it, carefully preserved, is the rose she wore. The principal speakers were the Lord Chief, Lord Houghton, Toole, and, of course, the guest of honour; the entertainers were Sims Reeves, Santley, and Antoinette Sterling. For days the papers were full of nothing else, and the comic journals blossomed into atrocious puns. The worst of these accompanied a picture of the Ghost of Shakespeare waking Irving up in the middle of the night and asking him if he proposed to play Malvolio in A-merry-key.

Then there is a break in the spate of heroic admiration whilst the compiler records the enthusiasm let loose by the first performance of *The Mikado*—a character and a country which Gilbert evoked out of his inner consciousness as the German professor did the camel. But this is a rare lapse, and the Irving-Terry duet is resumed, to be broken again by an account of the Bancrofts' farewell. It would almost seem as if the theatre of those days ranked more importantly than it does now. Here, for example, is a four-column "notice" of the production of *Faust*. Four columns, each containing a thousand words! As I read my blood tingles again. Alas that cold print can never reproduce the look, the voice, the anguish in the heart of Ellen Terry as she spoke the words:

> "To-morrow I must die,
> And I must tell thee how to range the graves,
> My mother the best place—next her my brother,
> Me well apart, but, dearest, not too far,
> And by my side my little one shall lie."

"No one who ever heard it will willingly forget the sweetness Miss Terry imparted to this passage." No one has forgotten it. The whole art of our tenderest actress is summed up in that "But, dearest, not too far." The scrapbook ends with the death of Irving. And I imagine that never was account of ceremony at the Abbey pasted in scrapbook with heavier heart.

(1924)

133

Let Us Meander

ASK one hundred people who was the author of the phrase "Let us have no meandering!" and one hundred people will reply: "Charles Dickens." Ask them what character of Charles Dickens said it, and ninety-nine will answer: "Betsey Trotwood." They will be wrong. The phrase was uttered by the old lady with the handbasket who, on the second page of *David Copperfield*, becomes the possessor of David's caul. I gather that that old lady would never have been a dramatic critic, since that functionary looks upon meandering very much as Alpine climbers look upon their rope. The rope will be there if it is wanted, and when the dramatic critic has nothing to say he can meander. Some writers, among whom Jules Lemaître stands out conspicuously, have won praise for their meandering—"Never is he more charming than when he digresses." This is Christmastime and I am in the mood that Hazlitt was in when he began the essay *On Living to One's Self* with the words: "I have a partridge getting ready for my supper, my fire is blazing on the hearth, the air is mild for the season of the year, I have had but a slight fit of indigestion to-day. . . ." My partridge has been gotten ready, only it was turkey, and has been eaten; but my electric stove still blazes, the evening air is mild, and I have no indigestion at all. Just as Hazlitt was never in a better place or humour for writing, so I know my poor self never to have been in finer fettle for meandering. First, then, let me suggest that there may be more virtue in literary meandering than is generally recognised. Some little time ago an unknown but, I am persuaded, charming friend sent me three tattered, paper-backed volumes, these being three-quarters of the *Memoirs* of Ernest Legouvé. Now, it may be that these most entertaining lucubrations are the common property of mankind in the sense that everybody has them on his bookshelves and if so disposed may take them down and read them for himself. But I confess that I am a little tired of people who object to quotations from forgotten writers on the plea that they have them under hand and can turn them up for themselves. My view is that not six people in London, and not two in the country, possess these *Memoirs*, and that one of the duties of the critic is to pass on some of the entertainment he has encountered in the course of his labours.

Legouvé's most interesting chapters are those which concern the great actress, Rachel, for whom he and Scribe wrote the famous *Adrienne Lecouvreur*, for many years the standby of Sarah Bernhardt, not disdained by Duse, and always a test piece for any actress pretending to virtuosity. Eugène Scribe, who was the senior partner in the collaboration, is out of fashion now, and I have hardly seen mention of him since Walkley devoted to him one of his ever-delightful Wednesdays. Nor, to tell the truth, have I, since he died, seen much mention of Walkley himself. He was scurvily treated by the obituary-mongers, though ten times wittier than Gosse, to whom those indiscriminate gentlemen devoted ten times the space. Hear Walkley's epitome of any play by Scribe: "The young marquis, ruined at cards, but an accomplished horseman, married the banker's daughter." Again: "Scribe's great success . . . was the result of three things—a natural instinct for the business [play-writing], industry and skill in meeting a popular demand, and a certain mediocrity of mind." And, of course, Walkley did not forget to quote the last gibe of Heine against the styleless successful mediocrity: "Pouvez-vous siffler?" the dying poet was asked. And he replied: "Pas même une comédie de M. Scribe!"

Legouvé's account of how *Adrienne Lecouvreur* was very nearly rejected by Rachel throws an amusing light upon that capriciousness which is the first characteristic of all great players. "The piece", he writes, "was composed at the request of Mlle Rachel. I may even say that she implored us to write it." The next sentence is quite untranslateable: "Mais les quelques mois que nous employâmes á écrire la pièce, Mlle Rachel les employa à s'en dégoûter." The day arrived for the reading of the piece, and everybody connected with the *Comédie française*, all the hangers-on of the great actress, and finally the great actress herself, turned up. It was known that Rachel did not want to play the part, and it was obvious that everybody who was to pass judgment upon the piece was determined to take his cue from the attitude adopted by Rachel. It was Scribe who read, and read badly, while Legouvé watched the proceedings from an armchair. Throughout the entire reading the actress's countenance showed no sign of interest, the judges' likewise. In Legouvé's words: "Pendant ces cinq longs actes, elle ne sourit pas, elle n'applaudit pas, elle n'approuva pas; ils n'approuvèrent pas, ils n'applaudirent pas, ils ne sourirent pas." Ultimately the committee informed the collaborators that Rachel did not see herself in the part. The following day three other managers made offers for the piece. But Legouvé was firm. The piece was written for the *Comédie française* and Rachel, and must be played at the *Comédie française* and by Rachel. At this juncture a new director was appointed to the theatre, and Legouvé insisted with him that the piece should be read again. The director consented, and the ceremony was repeated, Scribe absenting himself and Legouvé doing the reading. And then a delicious comedy took place. Throughout the first act Rachel smiled, applauded, and was obviously as much delighted with the piece as she had previously been disappointed. Why? For the simple reason that Rachel's excuse for rejecting the piece was not that it was bad, but that the role of Adrienne did not please her, *and Adrienne does not appear in the first act*. But here Rachel overreached herself, for her sycophants, seeing that she was pleased, threw themselves into raptures, with the result that the great actress was, despite herself, carried away on the wave of general emotion. The end of the reading found Rachel in floods of tears and hysterically enthusiastic.

But even before the first reading the collaborators had shown their play to a third person. "On the 5th of June 1879", wrote Legouvé, "there died in Paris at the age of eighty-four an old man of whose birth and death the public was first informed through the obituary notices." The old man was called Monsieur Mahérault. In the large world he had been a politician of small note; in the small world of the theatre he had been a play-doctor of great fame. In his capacity of dramatic adviser Mahérault had two admirable qualities. He never advised a playwright to do anything beyond his powers, and he pushed that playwright's talent along its own lines and nobody else's. The old man's verdict upon Scribe and Legouvé's play was that it was a character short. Scribe contested this, protesting that there was no room for an extra personage. Mahérault replied that his suggestion was not that the piece should have an extra character, but that an inconsiderable Duc d'Aumont who wandered through the play should be replaced by a personage of greater significance and closer to the period, say a little abbé. "Admirable!" cried Scribe. "An actress, a princess, a hero, and an abbé—there's our eighteenth century!" Legouvé also was quickly enamoured of the new character, of whom he writes: "La galanterie, le caquetage, l'amour, tout prit couleur dans sa bouche, et il courut, il bourdonna à travers la pièce, comme une chose ailée." The little abbé, in short, made the piece. Probably, if one took the trouble to wade through Sardou's pasteboard reproductions of dead-and-gone empires and civilisations, one would find that each play contained its equivalent of Mahérault's little abbé. One learned at school that for the success of certain chemical combinations the presence of a particular element is necessary; nothing, apparently, happens to the element, but without it the other parties to the transaction refuse to function. The little abbé and his like have always fulfilled the same office for Scribe, Sardou and other makers of the well-made play. They can be, and it is even better that they should be, subsidiary personages, and it is their business not so much to help the action as to be real. Give them reality, and they invest with that quality every creature surrounding them, or every personage round whom, as Scribe said, they buzz. Recognition of this fact is part of the equipment of every Frenchman of the theatre. M. Sacha Guitry has just made a gramophone record out of some random philosophic reflections upon most things under the sun, in the course of which he says:

"Quand une réplique, une phrase au théâtre est bien vraie et qu'elle est bien dite, en un instant les murs du décor sont en pierre, des gens habitent au-dessus, des voitures passent dans la rue, et derrière la porte de droit il y a un couloir, des chambres, une salle de bain, une cuisine, un escalier de service."

One touch of the natural knits the play, the players, and the period together—in a word, makes the whole theatre kin.

(1938)

White Kid Gloves

I was making my way to the Haymarket *première* when the awful thought occurred to me that I was improperly dressed. Conscience, after all, is the most implacable of sergeant-majors. I "went over" myself carefully. Yes, the hat was all right, a trifle less glossy than when, five seasons ago, Messrs. Shappo and Tile first placed it on my brow, but still indubitably a topper. The boots, a trifle undecided about the welt and, in places, cracked as handsomely as an old master's canvas, were yet of patent leather. Nor could reproach be levelled at that which came between. Were, perchance, my buttonholes something split? They belonged triumphantly to shirt and not to dicky. Were my cuffs frayed? At least they were not detachable. Was my customary suit of solemn black rustier than the waiter's at a dingy night club? Were the trousers more ragged than the temper of his proprietor after a raid? But theatre stalls hide a multitude of sins, including the seedy garb of your indigent dramatic critic. The overcoat and the mercerised muffler would be safely hidden in the cloakroom. Yes, all of me was right, in intention if not in effect. And yet, as I shivered on the top of the bus, I felt that something was wrong. It was not until I breathed hard into my blue hands that the fault dawned upon me. They lacked the white kid gloves proper to the correct appreciation of Mr. Barrymore's *Hamlet*.

Let it not be thought that there is not the subtlest philosophy here. There is. No woman would have eyes for an actor who should be Kean, Talma, Salvini, and Irving rolled into one, if she were conscious that her bodice had been buttoned awry. (It may be that bodices are no longer the mode, and that buttoning is as much out of date as ladylike behaviour at the theatre. Was it not a trifle tactless of the little lady next to me to be so very busy with lipstick and powder-puff just as Mr. Barrymore was telling her to what favour she must come at last?) No woman will think an actor all right who knows that her dress is all wrong. And why should man be made of sterner stuff? The pretence is pure pose.

Some time ago, having been telephoned for in accordance with the thirteen-at-table rule, I attended a dinner-party composed almost entirely of celebrities. The guests included a great writer, a suave boxer, a pugnacious bishop, a jockey, two popular actors—one of whom can really act—a great surgeon, an hotel proprietor, an All-England half-back, a lord, and some rubbish. Compliments were showered on a great football player, but he heeded them not. He sat gloomily, his brow clouded with thought. For he had lost the enamel out of one of his dress studs. The great writer, too, was out of temper, and had no smiles for all the nice things which were said about his latest satire, *Picanthropic Polly*. For the waiter had no knack in the way of serving soup, and on the great writer's shirt front appeared a map of Russia outlined in admirable Bortsch. Yes, we know what we are—as Ophelia says—but know not what we may be under the influence of trifling accident. Insignificant catastrophe had spoilt the evening for two men of genius.

To get oneself up in extraordinary fashion before attending the playhouse does not lack the sanction of precedent. The crowd assembling outside the doors of the *Théâtre français* at three o'clock on 25th February 1830 contained all the young men who were to become famous in the world of art. The occasion was the first performance of Victor Hugo's *Hernani*, and in the throng were Balzac, Berlioz, Théophile Gautier, Gérard de Nerval, Piccini, and a hundred lesser folk. The costume worn by Théophile Gautier has become historic. It consisted of a black spencer with velvet facings, pearl-grey pantaloons with stripes of black velvet, and a brilliant scarlet waistcoat which was to symbolise the defiant challenge of the new Romanticism. On the poet's feet were bright yellow shoes, and on his head was an immense sombrero with a high crown and a broad brim. In addition, it must be remembered that Gautier possessed a head of chestnut curls which came down to his waist. And in this extraordinary rig-out the author of *Mademoiselle de Maupin* awaited the opening of the door which was to let loose the Renaissance flood of strong words and strong action. Now, Gautier was a great man and, as such, neither nincompoop nor popinjay. There can be no doubt that he donned that blazing livery "to hear better". Molière poked fun at his old burgess for putting on his dressing-gown to the same intention: he would not have laughed at Gautier.

Nor, I think, would the old writer have deemed it ridiculous on my part to descend from the bus, make my way to a haberdasher's, and there lay out twelve shillings and sixpence on sheer, unnecessary magnificence. That pair of white kid gloves gave me delight in apprehension and confidence in judgment. I clutched them tightly throughout the performance, knowing that, so long as I did this, the great actor could not fail. Next morning, contrary to custom, I read my colleagues' criticisms of the play. And I knew at once which of them had sported white kid gloves, and which not.

White kid gloves play a notable part in all the joyful functions of life. (Lavender is the wear for marriage, but then one understands that that function is not wholly joyful.) I well recall my first pair. The occasion was the Manchester Jubilee Exhibition of 1887. I remember that I wore a kind of sailor's pea-jacket with twelve gold buttons, a white vest with six gold buttons, and a cap with "H.M.S. Invincible" in gold letters. I seem to recollect a lanyard with a whistle at the end, and certain heraldic devices on the sleeves—anchors, spinnakers, jibbooms. Lower down my costume was definitely childish—an affair of knickerbockers, well-scrubbed knees, cream socks, and patent-leather shoes fastened by a strap and button. Add to all this a pair of white kid gloves, and the reader will realise what a little monstrosity I looked.

In this rig-out I contrived to edge myself quite close to the Prince and Princess of Wales. The Prince wore an ordinary frock coat, and the glossiest top hat I had then beheld, its sheen far exceeding anything to be observed at Sunday-morning chapel. (We are a Dissenting family. I had four brothers, and Solomon in all his glory never filled Sunday-morning pew with such radiance as that given forth by our four pea-jackets, four white vests, and the seventy-two gold buttons.) But to return to the Royal Family. This was the first time I had seen the Princess of Wales, and something of the awe and wonder which her presence inspired is with me still. Whenever, in the play, Cleopatra bids the slave give better description of her rival Octavia:

"What majesty is in her gait? Remember,
If e'er thou look'dst on majesty"—

whenever I see an actress playing Cleopatra draw herself up to the most of her inches, I think then on a childish impression of forty years ago. The Princess wore a dove-coloured dress, and there was that air of grace and gentleness, of preening and plumage, about her which went far to mitigate awe. One wants a word for the passionate worship which should also describe the adoration of the child for a beautiful

140

picture hanging above his cot. The Prince spoke to me, but that was nothing. It was a word from his Princess that I wanted—and I had to be content with a smile. All that happened that day is still vivid in my memory. I remember that there was a luncheon, at which I was allowed to drink a little claret and water, that a scarlet band played, and presently we went to look at some pictures. I was bidden to admire one called "Diana or Christ?" and I was tremendously perturbed at being unable to discover which figure in the painting was which. I know that the Exhibition was very crowded, and at last I got a headache. But it was my heart which ached most—ached for the beautiful Princess. How desperately I wished to do her loyal service! To die would have been ideal. Yes, my first recollection of white kid gloves is mingled with ecstasy and agony. . . .

Too much fuss is made by novelists of the frock which the heroine wears at her first ball. Is not the hero's first dress suit of equal importance? I remember mine. To my infinite chagrin, it was only semidress. That is to say that I was allowed to sport an evening waistcoat, showing two mother-of-pearl studs, but the coat had to be of such cut that it could also be worn on Sunday mornings. Practice enabled one to throw back the lapels in such a way that when one was seated the dual purpose of the garment was not apparent. And then what difficulty one had with one's shirt front, which would crumple and "go in"! Manchester never showed its provincialism more strongly than in this matter of laundering dress shirts. Many were the devices that one tried, including stuffing with pocket-handkerchiefs, but it was not till one came to London that one could attain a grandeur in shirt fronts like unto that of Mr. Ben Davies. Well, too, do I remember the setting out to parties in yellow cabs. There were no india-rubber tyres in those days, and the vehicles made rattlesome progress over the cobblestones. But in the child's mind one question rose above the din—was it correct to put on one's gloves in the cab? And what if they should split? A young gentleman of my acquaintance taking two pairs, in case of disaster, such prodigality profoundly shocked the Northern mind, and young George was held up as an awful example of the young man who would one day emigrate to London and go to the bad. (In the provincial mind the two things are identical.) Well, George did actually go to the bad. He began by taking an amateur's interest in musical comedy, and ended by taking a financial one. I saw George a week or so ago, but he did not see me. I was creeping humbly into George's theatre when his six-cylinder Chrysler drew up and bespattered me with mud. A flunkey sprang from the chauffeur's side and opened the door. But it was George who handed out a bediamonded lady. And George's hand was covered with white kid.

(1924)

An Evening at Collins's

~~~~~~

THERE is nothing of listless, well-bred indifference in a visit to Collins's;
you must be prepared to take the red plush benches by storm. I like to
watch the curtain go up, having first enjoyed my fill of its bewitching
advertisements. I like to watch the musicians file in, to see the flute
player put his instrument together, and that honest workman, the
double-bass, spit on his hands, as all honest workmen should. I adore
the operation of tuning-up, the precision of those little runs and
trills executed in as perfect light-heartedness as the golfer's preliminary
swing. The conductor at these places is a captivating personage; he
epitomises the glory of suburbia—dinner jacket, "dicky", and white,
ready-made bow. The overture was entitled "The Woodbine Willie
Two-Step". Followed turns of which, or of whom, the chief were a
juggler striking matches on his skull, a stout lady with a thin voice,
prima donna of some undisclosed opera company, and a Versatile
Comedy Four having to do with bicycles. At length and at last comes
Mr. George Carney.

The first of his two "song-scenas" is a study of grandeur and deca-
dence, of magnificence on its last legs, dandyism in the gutter, pride
surviving its fall; in plain English, a tale of that wreckage of the Embankment which was once a gentleman. He wears a morning coat
which, in spite of irremediable tatters, has obviously known the sunshine of Piccadilly, has yet some hang of nobility. The torn trousers
still wear their plaid with an air. *Enfin*, the fellow was at one time gloved
and booted. There is something authentic, something inherited, something ghostly about this seedy figure. Trailing clouds of glory does he
haunt the Embankment. The ebony cane, the eyeglass with the
watered ribbon, the grey topper of the wide and curling brim—all
these fond accoutrements of fashion bring back the delightful 'nineties,
so closely are they the presentment, the counterfeit presentment, of the
swell of those days. "Bancroft to the life," we mutter. And our mind
goes back to that bygone London of violet nights and softly-jingling
hansom cabs, discreet lacquer and harness of cheerful brass—nocturnes,
if ever such things were, in black and gold—the London of yellow
asters and green carnations; of a long-gloved *diseuse*, and in the photographer's window a delicious Mrs. Patrick Campbell eating something

dreadfully expensive off the same plate as Mr. George Alexander; of a hardworking Max with one volume of stern achievement and all Time before him; of a Café Royal where poets and not yet bookmakers forgathered; of a score of music halls which were not for the young person . . . But I am getting away from Mr. Carney.

The matter is not very much above our heads—something about a Count who has "taken the count". The purest stuff of the music hall, as a music-hall song should be. "There's a n'ole 'ere!" pipes with fierce glee the cherub bootblack, bending over the broken boots and abating in deference to the broken swell no jot of his Trade Union rate of "frippence". How it hurts, the contempt and raillery of this pitiless infant! *Enfant goguenard* if ever there was one, a capitalist in his small way, and with all the shopkeeper's scorn of failure. "There's a n'ole 'ere!" he insists, and we are reminded of Kipps's tempestuous friend, "a nactor-fellow". "Not a n'ole—an aperture, my dear fellow, an aperture," corrects the noble client; "the boots were patent, but the patent's expired." Here the Count drops his cigar, and indulges in unseemly scuffle with the urchin. "No, you don't," says the riper smoker, regaining possession, "that's how *I* got it." But the child has yet another arrow. "Landlady says as 'ow you've got to share beds wiv a dustman." But the shaft fails to wound; clearly our hero is of the Clincham mould to whom social distinctions are as "piffle before the wind". "Want a pyper?" goads the boy, and his client lays out his last remaining copper. He unfolds the sheets and instinctively his eye runs over the fashionable intelligence. "Know Colonel Br'th'l'pp at all?" he inquires. One recognises this as the delightful touch of the man of the world anxious to put a social inferior at his ease. Something after this manner, one imagines, Royalty. "Doing very well in Russia. Was up at Cambridge with his brother, the *elder* Br'th'l'pp, don't cher know." And so to babble of the day's gossip to the scornful child at his feet. The courtesy, I submit, of one man of polish to another.

Night falls, the river puts on its jewels, the result of a cunning arrangement of n'oles and n'apertures in the backcloth; it draws very cold. More pitiful than the accustomed heir of destitution, but with stiff upper lip, our *déclassé* shivers, draws his rags more closely about him and moves on.

But it is the second song which brings down the house. Here the actor appears as an Army cook, and at Islington we have all been Army cooks in our time. A couple of dixies, the stew in which is discoverable last week's "Dicky Dirt", talk of "jippo" and "the doings"—all the familiar traffic of the camp rises to the mind's eye and sets the house in a roar. We are not, we gather, in any theatre of war, but safely at home in halcyon, far-off training days. Almost you can hear the cheerful clatter of the canteen, the thud and rattle of the horse-lines. The wording of the song is in no sense precious.

"What was the tale the Colonel told the Adjutant,
    What did the Adjutant say to Major Brown?"

There is a chorus, also serving as *corps de ballet*, and consisting first of the inveterate grumbler who objects to the presence in his coffee of so harmless a beastie as a "drahned mahse"—the accent is a mixture of Devon and Berkshire with a dash of Cockney. Then comes the superior youth of ingratiating, behind-the-counter manner, the proud possessor, we feel sure, of a manicure set in ivory—does he not abstractedly polish his nails on the end of his towel? After him the "old sweat" who will neither die nor fade away, and lastly our rosy bootblack, now the dear brother-in-arms of the immortal Lew and Jakin. This nucleus of an Army has but a single mind: to know what has become of its blinking dinner. Many and various are their ways of putting it, and it appears that they are no more than messengers or forerunners of the cohorts pressing on their heels. But the cook beguiles their impatience.

"What did the Major whisper to the Captain?
    The Captain told the Subs to hand it down."

The cook is the slipshod, inefficient, imperturbable "bloke" we know so well; with him we are to rise to what Mr. Chesterton calls "the dazzling pinnacle of the commonplace". (I am not sure that this is not the best of all this author's fireworks; it is so stupendous a rocket that the stick has cleared the earth, never to return but to go on whirling around this planet for ever.) Mr. Carney is the embodiment of the commonplace civilian turned soldier. He is the cook who will drop into the stew all manner of unconsidered trifles—cigarette ash, match ends, articles of personal attire. He is the hero up to all the petty knavery and "scrounging" that may be going, who will "work dodges" with the worst of them, and, on one occasion, join with the best in such deeds—he would still call them "dodges"—as shall put terror into the hearts of a ten times outnumbering foe. Of that order of

145

heroic cooks which held Ypres. But it is part and parcel of this actor's
generalship that he will have no truck with heroics. Tell Mr. Carney
that he raises tears and he will make a mock of you. Or more probably
he will continue his song.

> "What did the Quartermaster tell the Sergeant?
> The Sergeant told the Corp'ril, it appears,
> The Corp'ril told the Private and the Private told his girl,
> Now she's looking for Mademoiselle from Armenteers."

Have I overglorified my subject, whose talent is not more remarkably expended than on a dixie and a soldier's ration of stew? Ah, but
was not always one of the great tests for comic acting the power to
throw a preternatural interest over the commonest objects of daily life?
"What," say you, pricking your ears at the familiar phrase, "surely
at this time of day you are not going to dish up that old stuff about
kitchen tables and constellatory importance, joint schools and Cassio-
peia's chair?" Oh, but I am, and let appositeness be my apology. "So
the gusto of Munden antiquates and ennobles what it touches. His
pots and his ladles are as grand and primal as the seething-pots and
hooks seen in old prophetic vision." Why should I not elevate, an' it
please me, Mr. Carney's pot and ladle to the same high category? I do
not ask you to see in this actor an image of primeval man lost in
wonder of the sun and stars, but I do ask you to believe that a tin of
"bully" contemplated by him amounts, or very nearly amounts, to a
Platonic idea. Grant at least that he understands a dixie in its quiddity.
It may be that in my estimate of this conscientious comedian I have
overshot the just mean. Well, granting that my little appraisement is
an error, it seems to me to be an error on the right side. I have a
comfortable feeling that Islington, at least, is with me, that I have a
solid popular backing. Collins's pit and stalls, circle and gallery would
have borne me out that the actor diffused a glow of sentiment "which
made the pulse of a crowded theatre beat like that of one man"; would
have probably agreed that he had "come in aid of the pulpit, doing
good to the moral heart of a people".

I do not think that in expanding Islington's approval I have misread
it. Its ecstatic handclapping and shouts of "Good ole George! Good ole
George!" cannot deceive an ear attuned to shades of applause. The
civilian on my left with the wound stripes on his sleeve is dumb with
appreciation. His lips are parted, his breath comes in short gasps, his

eyes are fixed on the stage, seeing and not seeing, his whole soul in some setting of the past. The soldier on my right, still in the Army's grip and not yet victim of the nostalgia to come—a very small fly in demobilisation's ointment, but there it is—is drunk, simply, uncomplicatedly drunk, with the lilt and swing of the tune. He rises half out of his seat, puts a steadying hand on my arm, and with the other wildly conducts the house now singing in chorus:

"What was the tale the Colonel told the Adjutant?
What did the Adjutant say to Major Brown?
What did the Major whisper to the Captain?
The Captain told the Subs to hand it down.
What did the Quartermaster tell the Sergeant?
The Sergeant told the Corp'ril, it appears,
The Corp'ril told the Private and the Private told his girl,
Now she's looking for Mademoiselle from Armenteers."

There is a limit to the number of recalls even the most grateful servant of the public may permit himself, and at last Mr. Carney is allowed to retire in favour of the next turn. But my friend on the right takes some little time to simmer down. "Good ole George!" he continues to mutter under his breath. "Oh, good *ole* George!" And as the tumblers who come next are a dull pair, I wend my way out.

(1922)

Criticism and Mrs. Pat

Looking into Sainte-Beuve the other day, I came across a passage which defines the attitude of the critic so exactly that I feel that it should be once more dragged into the light.

Doubtless, this phrase will provoke a number of protests from readers informing me that they never go to sleep without having read a chapter of this famous critic. To those, therefore, for whom Sainte-Beuve is a favourite bed-book, I tender my humble apologies. My excuse is that even to a diligent reader of current literary criticism it would appear that Sainte-Beuve is, in the horrid phrase, a back number. At least, I cannot put my hand on my heart and swear that I have met him these last ten years in any columns except those of Edmund Gosse and Walkley. The great critic pretends that his views upon criticism are those " d'un homme d'esprit et de tact qui avait vieilli dans le journalisme". Bur this is modesty, and one begs leave to think that Sainte-Beuve is talking in his own person. Here is the passage:

"A critic may with perfect honesty permit himself three kinds of critical judgment. First there is his own private judgment to be delivered between four walls and to intimate friends. This judgment will necessarily take on the colour of the critic's own talent; consequently it will be personal, impulsive, quick, enthusiastic or severe, apt to make or mar. The note of such a judgment is predilection or antipathy.

"But one is not the only person in the world, nor can one claim to be the universal model; opinion may follow other forms of beauty besides that which appeals to the critic as being the nearest to his ideal. These other forms have the right to exist; and to enter into understanding of them it is necessary that the critic shall put himself on one side and even think against his own grain.

"The judgment arrived at after this compromise is the judgment which one should offer to the public since it will be informed by equity and intelligence.

"Finally, there is a third kind. This kind is influenced, at least in the form it takes, by external circumstances, and is marked by lenience towards the thing criticised, and consideration for the author thereof on the score of his standing or otherwise. This is the judgment of indulgence."

Personally, I find it extremely hard to agree with Sainte-Beuve. Surely, the essence of good criticism is that it shall bear its sincerity on its face. What the reader wants to know is what the critic really thought, and there can be no greater impertinence than that offered to critics at every dinner-party. "Of course, I saw what you wrote about *Papa's Gone a-Hunting!*" your fair neighbour will say; "but tell me, what did you really think?" The first-rate critic is one who convinces the reader that he wrote the truth as it appeared to him, the whole truth, and nothing but the truth. You knew what Montague felt about *The Belle of New York* when he wrote: "From a sympathetic presentation of a young hero drunk and lying on his stomach on the saddle of a bicycle and paddling in the air with his legs, the whole thing seemed to pass into an ecstatic fantasia on sex questions as these might be understood in fowl-runs or by cats in our backyards. The power of the play, as an emetic, was so great that I can only speak, as an eye-witness, of its first half." You knew what Mr. Shaw meant when he said of *True Blue: a New and Original Drama of the Royal Navy*, in an article with the title "Boiled Heroine": "One of the unnamed authors of this play is clearly an idiot." When Mr. Max Beerbohm said of Duse when she played Hedda Gabler that "apart from a general air of listlessness, like that of a guardian angel half asleep at her post over humanity, the actress showed not a shadow of comprehension of her part"—why, then you had some general inkling as to what Max thought of Duse's performance. I could, but will not, continue indefinitely.

It seems to me that the moment the critic takes anybody except himself into account he begins to lose sincerity. Every article by every critic who is allowed any space at all has a total gesture which is at once the sum of everything contained in that article, but is also something more than, and different from, that sum. You could call it, according as the critic pleases or displeases you, an aroma or a stench. In fact, every good critic tells you a good deal about himself, though he writes ostensibly, and even actually, only about other people. (I know, for example, a great deal about Mr. Bernard Darwin's golf because of what he makes me feel about James Braid's.) Should not, then, the corrections of private and personal judgment, which Sainte-Beuve says should be made by the critic, be made by the public reading him? I should not at any time have expected Montague to like *The Belle of*

New York. Like many exquisite writers, he had no ear for music, and frequently disclaimed expertness in musical matters. The whole point about this best of musical comedies is that it conquered in spite of its appalling vulgarity, and purely because of the entrancing tunefulness in which that vulgarity was clothed. I should not expect Mr. Shaw to like any tale told by an idiot, but I should have taken care to judge not from his verdict upon the naval melodrama, but from the facts stated in his article whether the play had been one of the amusing or one of the dull tales which can be told by idiots. I know enough of Mr. Beerbohm's perspicacity to realise that if there had been any in Duse's performance, the critic of the *Saturday Review* would have detected it. Lastly, I do not know that I should at any time expect my young and sprightly colleague to deem Shakespeare a good playwright. No, on the whole, I cannot see that there is any justification for Sainte-Beuve's second category. As for the third type of judgment—that of indulgence —I hold with the utmost firmness and modesty that Sainte-Beuve is totally and completely wrong. No actor should be allowed to "get away with" a bad Macbeth because on a previous occasion he was a good Shylock.

Last week Mrs. Patrick Campbell, who is, by common consent, one of the greatest actresses of the last generation, appeared as Mrs. Alving in Ibsen's *Ghosts*. The theatre was crowded with young people anxious to see a great example of that art of acting which we are always preaching to them and is now no more than a legend. Mrs. Campbell had no sooner set foot upon the stage than one recognised that here was an art of talking, walking, looking, and being of which the actresses of to-day know nothing. I shall not expatiate further upon this; it must be enough if I say that for thirty-five years Mrs. Campbell has been, at any time when she has really wanted to be, among the finest half-dozen actresses in Europe. I shall take leave to apply to Mrs. Campbell's performance of Mrs. Alving Sainte-Beuve's first code of critical judgment, and to allow readers to make the necessary corrections. Let me begin by saying that I went to Wyndham's Theatre with the highest expectations, and for two acts sat in my stall in a condition which I can only describe as horrorstruck. For it seemed to me that, though the great actress was going through all the motions of great acting, she was not acting at all! Years ago Mr. Shaw wrote of Mrs. Campbell's performance in *The Notorious Mrs. Ebbsmith*: "She creates all sorts of illusions, and gives one all sorts of searching sensations. It is impossible not to feel that those haunting eyes are brooding on a momentous past, and the parted lips anticipating a thrilling, imminent future, whilst some enigmatic present must no less surely be working underneath all that subtle play of limb and stealthy intensity of tone. Clearly there must be a great tragedy some-where in the immediate neighbourhood: and most of my colleagues will no doubt tell us that this imaginary masterpiece is Mr. Pinero's *Notorious Mrs. Ebbsmith*. But Mr. Pinero has hardly anything to do with it. When the curtain comes down you are compelled to admit that, after all, nothing has come of it except your conviction that Mrs. Patrick Campbell is a wonderful woman." The fault there is imputed as clearly as possible to Mr. Pinero, who, to put it bluntly, had given Mrs. Campbell nothing to play. I had exactly the same sensation during last week's performance of Mrs. Alving. But it would be monstrous to suggest that Ibsen was giving the actress nothing to play; the part of Mrs. Alving contains as much as genius itself can cope with. In my view, the truth is simply this—that Mrs. Campbell's mind throughout those first two acts was anywhere and everywhere except in the play. You felt, in fact you knew, that there was a great tragedy somewhere in the immediate neighbourhood, and you asked yourself why, oh why, Mrs. Campbell didn't take the trouble to give it you. In the third act she recaptured our respect and compelled all our old admiration. One felt justified in telling the young people present that this was great acting, just as one had felt justified in telling them during the first and second intervals that their ecstasies were the effusions of inexperience talking through its hat.

(1928)

151

Looking and Leaping

ᔡᔡᔡᔡᔡᔡᔡᔡᔡᔡᔡᔡᔡᔡᔡᔡᔡᔡᔡᔡᔡᔡᔡᔡᔡᔡ

I HAD been asked by my newspaper to fly to Paris and record my impressions. Now, I have always been nervous about heights. Mountains terrify me, as do mastheads, lighthouses, upper floors—every form of human eyrie. I would not inhabit New York, that inferno of the somnambulist, for a Labour Leader's ransom. I cannot even suffer the gallery at the theatre. How fearful and dizzy 'tis to cast one's eyes so low! Methinks the actors seem no bigger than their heads. I always feel that in some fit of auto-hypnotism, some attack of sheer funk if you will, I shall throw my opera-glasses into the pit, and myself after them, in desperate retrieval. It is a common experience for men to dream that they fall, and wake before they reach the ground. I have two dreams in which I hark back to that dreadful recollection. One is of a schoolmate who, on a hot August night, stole from his dormitory to the cool swimming bath, which for some reason had been emptied, and dived . . .

The other concerns a climbing accident on the Pillar Rock. I suppose it must now be some thirty years ago; at least, it is so far distant that I can write of it without emotion, although there was a time when I could not have done so. Indeed, for a year or two afterwards not only the scarps and crags of Westmorland, but the rolling uplands of Yorkshire filled me with nervous dread. My friend and I—let me say at once that the accident was strictly none of our business, and that we came into it after it was all over—my friend and I had saved seven pounds each and resolved to expend them on a walking tour in the Lakes. On a Friday afternoon, preceding a Whitsun Bank Holiday of the early 'nineties, two youthful wayfarers "might have been observed" trudging on foot along the path which, skirting the lake of Derwentwater, brings the traveller into Borrowdale. Besides his knapsack, each carried his share of a cumbersome photographic apparatus with three legs. Kodaks, films, auto-developers, and all the newfangled rest of it, had not yet come into being. In those days one did one's own developing, printing, mounting, and scorned the common chemist. I remember that about this period one took in a quaint little weekly in which a Mr. Horsley Hinton was wont to descant upon the artistic possibilities of cotton-wool, with the aid of which you could do better than

Rembrandt. I am still proud of my view of Friar's Crag, or whatever the little peninsula is called which runs out into Derwentwater at so convenient an angle that the westering sun, casting his rays on the boles of the trees, turns them into pools of liquid gold. This is the view upon which the London and North-Western Railway principally relies to attract visitors to Lakeland. My version of it contains a boat in which my friend romantically sits, reading a tattered Pickwick. We have not met much during the last thirty years. Austen has given his life to a highly successful business, and a not quite so successful performance of the 'cello part in Brahms's quartets; mine has run to the stringing of sentences. Austen never leaves Manchester except under compulsion; I never return there except upon the like condition. Betaking myself thither a short time ago upon some business of lecturing, whom should I see in the front row but old Austen! I was well under way before my eye caught sight of his dear, satirical, mocking countenance. . . .

On my way to the train for London—since no man would sleep in Manchester for the pleasure of it—we had time for a word or two. We recalled Rosthwaite, and how we had spent that broiling Bank Holiday in the conquest of Great Gable, Scafell, and Scafell Pike, legging it wearily to Seascale as the sun went down. I have never been so tired in all my life as I was on that evening, recollection of that feat of boyish endurance enabling me to understand something of the courageous equipment of Arctic and Himalayan explorers. Twenty miles, you say, is not much of a march? Remember Einstein, dear reader, and get it into your noddle that fatigue is relative as much as anything else, and that to a growing boy twenty miles under a hot sun, with three mountains and the legs of a camera thrown in—dear, unselfish Austen, who carried the heavier case!—may prove pretty stiff. Next day we returned to Wastdale, and there, at the famous inn, we supped in company with two young men from London who, on the morrow, were to go out climbing. The talk turned naturally to that sport and its risks. Our friends were modest. They were no experts, they said, all of their experience having been obtained in the Isle of Skye during the previous fortnight. On their way south to rejoin their respective banks they had decided to bag a few Lakeland trophies. We went to bed at ten o'clock. The following evening the climbers failed to put in an appearance at dinner. Nine, ten, eleven o'clock, and still no sign of them. The people at the inn did not seem over-anxious, saying that climbers often mistook their way home and even made the descent into Ennerdale instead of Wastdale. They did, however, consult the guide, a Swiss who, on hearing that the young men had talked of the Pillar Rock, looked grave. There were only two of them, he remarked, and they had no more than twenty feet of rope, whereas for this expedition three climbers and thirty feet of rope are recognised as the proper thing. It was arranged that François should proceed early next morning to the Rock and report. After breakfast Austen and I, deciding for an easy day, sauntered a mile or two in the direction of the Pillar Mountain. Suddenly, from the top of a low hill, we saw the guide wave to us and start to run in our direction. We ran to meet him. From a distance of three-quarters of a mile he had seen the bodies of the two young men, roped together, hanging over the Rock.

We returned to the inn and made up the party for retrieval. Arrived within some three hundred yards of the Rock, the guide stopped and bade us go on, cut the rope, lay the first man on the stretcher, and bring him to the spot where we then stood, and where he, the guide, would remain. François refused to approach nearer; he would, he said, do more than his share of the carrying, but not one inch nearer the scene of the accident would he go. He must, he said, climb the Rock for a living; and if the Rock were haunted, as for him it would be if he meddled with its dead, he would be afraid to tackle it in the future and so would lose his employment. Upon this declaration we did as we were bid. At that time I had never seen a dead man, and to make this discovery under conditions of horror put a very great strain upon my nerves. The journey had to be made twice, and for the last mile we converted the stretcher into a rude sleigh pulled by a horse from a neighbouring farm. Nothing, I think, could have exceeded the impression made on me by that twilight cortège, the black horse dragging the shrouded figure, and the torches which we presently lighted. For some curious reason there had been few visitors at Wastdale at that particular holiday season, and Austen and I and the two bank clerks had been the last to remain. It was Austen who telegraphed to the parents and would hear of no softening of the news. Better, he said, the sudden shock than the daylong journey of hoping against hope.

It was Austen who met the boys' parents at the station and did what he could in the way of comfort, which was to listen. The poor folk seemed to want to talk, to unburden themselves about Willie and Tom, even to a stranger. So for hours Austen sat, an island of comfort around which the tide of this grief surged and wore itself out, at least for that day.

Since then I have had as little stomach for this sport as I have at any time had head. Yet climbers' books delight me, and the subject finds me full of lore. I believe I could hold my own in a mountaineers' talk by the fire; that is if I were sure of returning to town on the following morning. I am as familiar with some of the most famous climbs in the British Isles as though I had achieved them. I know the maximum angle at which snow will lie, the danger of grass slopes, the difference between the French and English meanings of the word "Alpinist." I can read every book about mountaineering that I can get hold of, and yet tremble at the ascent of Snowdon from Llanberis. The spirit is willing; it is the flesh, or at least the nerve-centre controlling fear, which is weak. Descents trouble me not at all. I can face with equanimity the coalmine and the submarine. "Facilis descensus Averno" was obviously written by a man with a poor head for heights. The upshot? I looked but did not leap.

(1923)